CROSSING
LINES

CROSSING LINES

Research and Policy Networks for Developing Country Education

Edited by Noel F. McGinn

Westport, Connecticut
London

Library of Congress Cataloging-in-Publication Data

Crossing lines : research and policy networks for developing country
   education / edited by Noel F. McGinn.
      p.   cm.
   Includes bibliographical references (p.   ) and indexes.
   ISBN 0-275-95511-7 (alk. paper)
      1. Education—Developing countries. 2. Communication in
   education—Developing countries. 3. Information networks—
   Developing countries. 4. Education—Research—Developing
   countries. I. McGinn, Noel F.
   LC2607.C76   1996
   370′.9172′4—dc20   95–53002

British Library Cataloguing in Publication Data is available.

Library of Congress Catalog Card Number: 95–53002
ISBN: 0–275–95511–7

First published in 1996

Praeger Publishers, 88 Post Road West, Westport, CT 06881
An imprint of Greenwood Publishing Group, Inc.

Printed in the United States of America

The paper used in this book complies with the
Permanent Paper Standard issued by the National
Information Standards Organization (Z39.48–1984).

10 9 8 7 6 5 4 3 2 1

CONTENTS

Contents   *vii*

PREFACE

Communication across boundaries and across the seas is so easy today and so widespread that we are tempted to presume that the formation and maintenance of systems of communications, the process called networking, began in our time. We may forget how during the nineteenth century news of advances in philosophy and science, and the arts and humanities as well, traveled quickly through the mails and by the migration of people. Domingo Sarmiento, for example, eager to bring to Argentina all the benefits of civilization, traveled throughout Europe and then the United States examining school systems and meeting leading educators. After returning to Argentina, he maintained his network through extensive correspondence, including more than twenty years of letter writing with the widow of Horace Mann. Information exchanged through the network had a marked impact on education policies in Argentina when Sarmiento was elected president. In the century before, Thomas Jefferson maintained a voluminous correspondence with leading intellectuals and politicians in Europe. Jefferson shared with his European colleagues information about flora and fauna found in what was to become the United States. In return he learned much about political philosophy in addition to the latest scientific theories and principles of engineering. The Declaration of Independence and the Constitution of the United States owe much to Jefferson's involvement in European networks.

Perhaps in many other centuries we could find one or more figures who stand out for their connectedness with others in their own and in other countries. And for each of those figures we could assume that there were many more who participated in active and widespread communication networks. However, it is characteristic of our knowledge that today we know only about the leading figures in those networks with some connection to our own country. I am ignorant, for example, about examples of earlier networks in Asia and Africa, even though I am certain that those networks existed even before the European Enlightenment and the Westernization of the world (Von Laue, 1987).

Communication between and among people is essential to the process of forming human society. It is the means by which members of a community learn those values, knowledge and skills that are essential to the survival and growth of the community, and that give meaning to individual life in a social context. Community permits humankind to advance more rapidly than the smartest, most inventive individual. It permits multiplication of effort, with eventual production of economic surplus that frees some persons to invent even better ways to meet our minimal requirements and to make sense of our existence.

That process by which knowledge appears and grows in more than one person is sometimes defined as the transmission or dissemination of innovation. The metaphor of dissemination implies a source of ideas and knowledge who spreads seeds that grow into predetermined forms when they germinate in fertile ground. An alternative metaphor is that of production, in which ideas and data are inputs transformed by receiving persons into a variety of things that cannot be anticipated.

These metaphors, and other ways of thinking about education, are much in discussion today, as the world considers whether the current technology of school-ing is the best way to go about forming and changing communities. In one sense the school classroom is a network with a source linked to the outside (through curriculum and supervisors) that encourages communication among students but primarily between students and teacher. The schooling model is designed to transmit or disseminate knowledge produced elsewhere. Our research on schooling is, for the most part, designed to tell us how to make the model work better than it does now. At the same time, however, some are questioning whether schooling can be made to work much better than it does now, or whether we have pushed the technology to the limits of its capabilities.

This is a worldwide question. All education systems seem to be under question. Much welcomed, then, are technological advances that (for some of us) make it possible to build more and more networks that link us together, facilitating a greater flow of information about experiences with education. What distinguishes our communication today from that of previous centuries is its extensiveness. It is possible now to talk of global networks.

Many of the new networks being formed, like those of previous centuries, link those who do research on education with persons who make decisions and policies that affect how education systems operate. This connection may have been com-mon in earlier centuries, but diminished in the first half of the twentieth century as science under the positivist model developed increasingly specialized language in each discipline. Concern for reconnecting science and politics mounted after World War II, leading to research on the utilization of scientific knowledge.

The networks discussed in this book are the children of that concern, spawned by a hope that the application of scientific knowledge to our education systems can remedy the problems we experience. Our collective ability to overcome difficulties in communication between research producers and research users is not yet fully understood but certainly of high concern.

The chapters included in this book are addressed to all those participants in communication about education research who wish to improve their ability to communicate, and to construct and maintain systems of communication. This is a collection for people engaged in networking.

The contributions to this volume came through the Northern Research Review and Advisory Group (NORRAG), a network that seeks to improve communication between researchers, educators, and policy makers about education in the South. Some of the chapters first appeared in number 13 of the *NORRAG News*, dedicated to the topic of networking. Others were written for an annual general meeting of NORRAG held in Oxford, England in 1993.

The main objective of this collection is to (1) improve our understanding of how education research networks operate, (2) identify obstacles to effective operation, and (3) suggest methods for improvement of networking. Part I of the collection provides some elements for a framework to use in analysis of networks and networking. The remaining sections provide descriptions and critiques of the operation of various networks.

We have included a list of education research centers in networks in Asia and Latin America, and a list of network newsletters. There are also author and topic indexes.

The majority of the chapters deal with the experience of networking in Africa. This may be because the South East Asia Research, Review, and Advisory Group (SEARRAG) and Red Latinoamericana de Información y Documentación en Educación (REDUC), networks formed earlier in South East Asia and Latin America, respectively, have high levels of internal communication and therefore relatively less contact with NORRAG in the North, than do incipient networks in Africa. The issue of internal and external communication is addressed in several of the papers.

The perspective that knowledge is not transmitted, but instead produced in the mind of each person-as-knower as a result of interaction between the person and what is outside, makes it impossible to insist on one given concept of the purpose and effective operation of networks. Consistent with that perspective, this collection offers several views of what networks are and can be. Like many innovations, networks exist in multiple forms. What is appreciated is not the network itself, as (from this perspective) a network is an abstraction. What is appreciated is your unique experience of communication with others. The network you are in is different than the network they are in. Latin American networking is different than Asian networking which differs from the European variety (of which there could be more than one).

The challenge for us all is how to learn to communicate, to share information, and to mutually generate new knowledge across the cultural and professional boundaries that have separated us.

A CONCEPTUALIZATION OF
NETWORKS AND NETWORKING

PART I

The use of the term "networking" to refer to social communication followed shortly after adoption of the term in the early twentieth century to describe systems of physical objects such as canals, roadways, telephones, and radio transmitters and receivers. Carton suggests that there are two uses of the term: (1) networking as an action within a system of fixed routes and boundaries, and (2) networking as a process of creating linkages.

Carton sees this latter approach to networks as most appropriate for describing the process of globalization, which can be understood roughly as expansion of a network across boundaries. For quite some period of time, accelerating in the latter half of the twentieth century, human beings have expanded their communication networks to transcend families, local communities, and now nations. The effects and implications of this process are not fully understood, but appear to be profound.

Carton uses the metaphor of the multinational corporation to discuss the effects of globalization on the structure of networks. Multinationals have over the past twenty years made fundamental changes in their structures and operations. They have gone from being bounded systems with strong central control, to open systems with decentralized nodes of authority linked together through information networks.

Changes in the purposes and operations of networks are also the topic of the contribution by Lauglo. He proposes that networks have a "natural" history. Friends or like-minded persons carry out activities together. As the group grows, a newsletter is published. A forum may be next, followed by formalization of the network as an association. At the mature stage, networks offer their services to other groups.

Dubbeldam takes a broader perspective. He argues that some networks survive not because of formalization, but because those who participate in the network benefit from the relationship. Many networks emerge spontaneously, and may disappear as easily. Exchange of information is a central benefit to networking, but obstacles to information flow can choke off the progress of the network. Networks can contribute to development of the capacity of other organizations (i.e., institution building), but this requires other activities as well.

The role of information in networking is the central theme of the paper by King. The utility of information poses special problems for its flow within a network. While information may be neutral in itself, what we collect and distribute to others is conditioned by values. Policy makers may seek a different kind and content of information than that produced or amassed by a researcher. The value of information can lead to "hoarding," which over the long term would have destructive effects on a network. Information is shared to achieve some purpose, to advocate some position about problems and/or their solutions. Full exchange of information among all members of a network, each acting as a supplier and a consumer, insures the health of the network.

How can we evaluate the success of a network? Dubbeldam and King insist on information flow as the critical factor in the success of networks. It is important to distinguish, however, between the total volume of information a network can generate—which could be primarily the work of a few individuals—and the number and quality of exchanges among all the possible pairs of members. There is no evidence that any network does this latter kind of evaluation. What indicators of success could be used instead?

The chapters that follow imply (but do not develop) two possible indicators. The first is simple. People persist in networks to the extent that they are beneficial to them. If we assume that increased information is the primary personal gain that motivates networking, then stability and growth of membership of a network is prima facie evidence that it is working well. The second indicator is more complex. To the extent that communication leads to increased mutual understanding, a successful network will be characterized by more rather than less similarity of interests and concerns and language of members.

McGinn suggests that conditions of full exchange of information require (and are the product of) a culture of intimacy in the network. Hierarchical organizations attempt to improve communication flow through regulated standardization. Heterarchical and horizontal organizations work to increase intimacy. Constraints to intimacy include heterogeneity of membership, physical distance, and organizational size. Perhaps a more serious obstacle to intimacy is the view that information and knowledge are commodities rather than shared understandings that are constructed over and over again as people communicate.

The variety of newsletters and networks listed by King demonstrates the urgency many feel to communicate across boundaries.

FROM GROUP TO NETWORK:
SOCIOLOGICAL PERSPECTIVES

Michel Carton

As early as 1934, Moreno referred to "psycho-social networks of communication" to describe relationships that go beyond the boundaries of a group, and noted that even institutionalized groups have porous limits. In the 1970s, through the use of different instruments like graph theory and computers, the network approach passed from micro to macro social fields. The International Network for Social Network Analysis was created in 1978.

Today the term "network" is used in four different ways : (1) as a *material object* as in the technical, physical, and territorial fields of energy, transportation, and telecommunication; (2) as an *analytical tool* for a geographical, social, or economical situation whose structure or process can be formalized through different methods, such as graph theory; (3) as a *theoretical analytical object* at which one is looking to discover specific functioning laws, such as services; and (4) as a *social science concept*, such as a specific organization mode, the entrepreneurial organization of economic activities, and the managerial organization of public services.

Socially and politically speaking a network can be either an official, formal instrument of relationships between different actors (associations, public services) or an informal alternative to existing power structures. These definitions derive from British anthropological work of the 1950s which criticized the structural-functionalist approach as incapable of explaining the complex, specific, innovative ways in which urban societies already were evolving (Mitchell, 1969).

The critics took one of two positions with respect to networks: (1) For Bott (1971), social networks are informal groupings with fixed limits. In complex societies they are the equivalent of corporate groups found in "primitive" settings; (2) For Barnes (1969), social networks are a concept that allows us to visualize the multiple relations that go beyond the limits of specific groupings, as these relations are never stable and always diversifying.

Combining Bott's approach with Mitchell's study of networks raises five general questions for any social network:

1. What is its *density?* How many people are effectively in contact, in comparison with the ideal number which could/should be considered?
2. What are the *distances* between the members? How many people stand in between two people willing to communicate?
3. What is its *starting point:* an individual or a group?
4. What is the *social structure* of the membership? Is it diversified?
5. What do members *gain*, as a function of duration, frequency, and intensity of relationships?

Attempts to use these questions to define network typologies have been unsuccessful, according to Bott himself. Barnes's definition, which insists on the innovative, open-ended, and action- change-oriented characteristics of networks, is preferable. His is a strategic approach which distinguishes networks from structures organized, generally speaking, on a center-periphery hierarchical approach.

According to the French philosopher Serres (1968), "a network is, at a specific time (as it is a simple stage of a mobile situation), constituted of numerous points connected by numerous paths. By definition, no one point is privileged against another one." It is a model characterized by "the plurality and complexity of mediation paths: there is a great number of different ways to pass from one point to another one" (Serres 1968, pp. 11–12). In this definition, a network is nonhierarchical and without a center. Organizations which define themselves as networks linking individuals who belong to different institutional settings (development agencies, nongovernmental organizations [NGOs], universities) and who work in connected fields at different levels of research and action in many countries, are then close to the trend today followed by multinationals that have organized into "network firms."

When first started, multinational firms achieved high levels of efficiency through centralization, and displaced local firms. Now the globalization process has generated sociogeographical economic zones that tend to be self-centered. The European Common Market is one example. To maintain efficiency, multinational corporations have to decentralize, at least to the level of the economic regions. Efficiency is maintained by the externalization of different costs toward other enterprises and institutions (private and public, like universities) through agreements and contracts. Horizontal local structures are intended to permit the multinational to adapt to regional changes in consumption patterns and technology. The network approach is a feasible means to permit the multinational firm to maintain efficiency and integrity by transcending the exclusivity of the economic zones.

But the question of the existence of a center-periphery process is still open: can a network function without a center? And whatever the answer is, what are the boundaries of the periphery?

These different considerations perhaps have kept researchers from looking at networks not only as a way to increase the productivity of different types of production and communication processes but also as powerful instruments for institutional development. In this regard, the work of the Swiss sociologist Meister, who worked for twenty years on the different participatory conceptions and schemes used in the North and in the South, is important. He makes a clear distinction between "provoked-planned" participation and "spontaneous" participation (Meister, 1978).

It is clear that many networks have been set up by different kinds of organizations, public and private, to externalize, for example, a critical function which was too expensive or risky to develop or maintain within their structures: it is a kind of provoked-planned participation process where the actors are at the same time dependent on and autonomous of their sponsors. Some other networks are set up in a spontaneous way by which some individuals or groups try to influence one or many organizations.

Some organizations may have elements of both planned and spontaneous development. This ambivalent and ambiguous position can be considered as dangerous. Fifty years ago, Gramsci noted the problem posed by the situation and role of the intellectual with respect to organizations (Hoare and Smith, 1971).

A specific aspect of the network approach refers to the situation in which some states—represented by their administration as well as by their education system, including the university—are based on a balance between clientelism and legalism. Too often in the South the balance is in favor of clientelism. In the North the opposite is supposed to be the case (Bayart, 1989). In these cases, concerned people belonging to state organizations launch networks not with the intention of transcending institutional boundaries, but instead to force institutions to define their territories and limits in a more legal, efficient, and bureaucratic manner. Such networks often are composed of people from public research, practice, and policy settings; they contribute both to policy discussions (by initiating or backing them) and to project implementation (research and/or action). Participation in implementation is required because of lack of action by education authorities, often due to the imbalance between their legal and clientelist dimensions. The question of the role of the state or center of power is then clearly at stake in this discussion about networks.

Finally, coming back to the individuals who constitute a network, the following functions at the personal level can be distinguished, based on the assumption that every member carries knowledge, experiences, values, information, and strategies:

identity—belonging to a network is an extension of the identity of the member

support—belonging to a network is a psychological, material, and strategic support for decision making

necessity—belonging to a network is a necessity allowing individuals to go beyond their individual limits *equality*—a network is not a competition/conflict organization system, under the condition that rules are clear

cooperation—sharing of information is the main objective

Based on these characteristics, the management of a network with both individual and social dimensions, and functional and critical objectives, will aim to facilitate (1) the collection, analysis, and interpretation of messages to disseminate, (2) the improvement of internal relations, and (3) the definition of common projects and objectives.

EVOLUTION OF NETWORKS:
EVOLUTION FROM NETWORKS

Jon Lauglo

The network analogue applied to professional relations evokes diverse associations, such as, network as a web, power networks, and professionals in networks.

The network as a web has numerous strands with interconnecting points (knots), a great many knots, each one connected directly to just a few others, but indirectly to all others through chains of intermediate points. Such a web, once put into place, is a static structure which gives strength to resist wear and tear.

There are several varieties of power networks:

> *Single source*—Energy is generated at one central point and diffused through numerous intermediate transmission points to a large number of ultimate consumers of energy. For example, a single radio transmitter (or electricity station), numerous transformers or transponders, and a great many ultimate outlets at which energy is used.

> *Power grid*—Energy is generated at several points. These are interconnected at several points to maintain the total flow of power to a large grid that reaches out to numerous receivers through a series of mediating transformers or transponders.

> *Interactive networks*—All points generate and receive energy. Some points generate more energy and transmit directly or indirectly to a greater number of receivers than do others. But interactive networks are distinguished from other forms by each point being a transmitter as well as a mediator and receiver.

Professionals are plugged into diverse networks. Some may be akin to the stable web, but most important are the power networks through which energy or information flows: new knowledge, ideas, and awareness of resources into which one can tap. The extent to which professionals are centrally or peripherally placed in such networks in terms of energy received, depends on the extent to which you make contributions which others value. If you are famous, you receive not only requests for reprints but numerous unsolicited papers that others write.

It also helps to be close to centrally placed persons. Underlings and departmental colleagues share in the stream of communication that a more centrally placed person receives. But his or her interest in sharing depends in the long run on whether there is much value in the returns received.

If you control resources (e.g., can commission research and consultancies, invite others to conferences, or sit on editorial boards) you receive more "energy" from others than if you are not perceived to have such influence. Of course, the importance of having good networks is not new, nor does it require modern telecommunications. Witness the extensive international correspondence of Thomas Jefferson.

Within a professional field, the network creating agencies that traditionally have been influential are training institutions, professional associations with their committees and conferences, and professional journals. What is new today is the attention given to building networks by additional means and the emphasis on interactive networks, where in order to belong you also have to contribute—a bit like a seminar with participants based in different locations.

Typically what happens is the following: A centrally placed professional gets access to resources which makes it possible to invite others to a workshop on a chosen team. All participants are to contribute. A network project is formed with intentions to meet again on future dates for renewed sharing of contributions. Such a project is primarily an information sharing activity which depends crucially on the initiator's entrepreneurship and ability to generate funding for the network and to reach out and involve a core of colleagues who are also well known in the field. It will thus have more of a proprietary character and be more exclusive in its membership (limited to active contributors) than a professional association.

After the initial flash of getting-together activity, which professionals working on related themes value in its own right, networks can probably only survive in the long term if they take on more focused tasks that make them resemble other types of organizations. For example, a joint research project may spring from a network. To those who provide the financing, the proof of the pudding will then lie in the quality of the project. Medium-term survival follows if the project turns into a major research program (e.g., the International Education Achievement [IEA] studies). But the organizational form will change to reflect the changing focus from network project to research program. It is perhaps especially in this respect that international network projects have a real mission. It is organizationally complicated and expensive to plan international research projects. Something akin to an especially funded network project is often needed to take ideas for such research forward. Even so, if networks are to generate such work they need to have a fairly sharp thematic focus to begin with and they need to include outstanding individual researchers in the countries which are to participate.

Then, a newsletter develops to service the network internally and to advertise its existence externally in order to draw attention to it, attract new applicants for future events, and keep sources of finance happy. Insofar as the newsletter evolves into a professionally valuable publication available to subscribers, the network becomes a circle of professionals with a strong interest in promoting the evolving journal. There will be an editorial board and a larger circle of regular contributors.

The meetings become a major forum for presenting research. The network then evolves into a professional association (and may include the development of a journal), with a larger and more open membership than the original network, and with leadership evolving into less proprietary forms. This is more likely to happen when previously existing professional fora are weakly developed in the thematic niche of the network, and when that niche is large enough to sustain regular conferences.

Finally, the network is sustained as a marketing device for a consulting firm, which generates needed funding from the sale of its services. In this case, the proprietary organizational form of the network becomes formalized in a firm.

Thus, the argument presented here, admittedly based more on a hunch than on data, is that those activities which are launched as network projects tend to be transitory, like all projects. Networks require special funding. The entrepreneurs who succeed in obtaining such funding will naturally initially lead and direct the activities of the networks. Networks have short-term value in bringing professionals more closely together (and in more direct ways, e.g., e-mail) than normal professional associations usually do. Compared to professional associations they also have narrower themes. By doing so they may be the cradle of more focused and hence more sustainable activities, such as research programs, journals, professional associations, or consulting firms.

NETWORKS AND INSTITUTION BUILDING

Leo F. Dubbeldam

DEFINITIONS

Network

A network is "an arrangement of parallel wires etc. crossed at intervals by others so as to leave open spaces; anything like this, as a system of interconnected roads, individuals; radio and TV, a chain of transmitting stations" (Guralnik, 1976, p. 966) or "a large number of people, groups or institutions, etc. that have a connection with each other and work together as a system" (Hanks, 1979, p. 403). As Carton notes in "Sociological Perspectives," the term "network" can be used as material object, an analytical tool, a theoretical analytical object, or as a social science concept.

In this chapter, network is meant as the pattern of social contacts of an individual through which she or he can achieve information, support, credits, power, and other essentials needed for survival or for improvement of one's position. At a certain point, "individual" can be exchanged for "institution."

Institution Building

While the dictionaries are clear about what a network is, they are less so when an institution is defined. There seems to be some agreement that it is a (large and important) organization having a public, social, educational, or religious purpose, for example, a university, a church, or a bank. In principle this embraces government, parastatal, academic, research and training institutes, private organizations, and professional organizations. It seems that a legal basis for the organization is essential. Institutional development and institution building refer to efforts to establish or strengthen such organizations.

Networking

Networking has meaning at different levels and types of social interaction between people. There is one element that all networks share: they imply multiple, in principle reciprocal, contacts between individuals (or institutions). The examples that follow illustrate this point.

In anthropological literature the Kula trade is well known (Piddington, 1950; Malinowski, 1950). The Kula is an institution found among peoples who inhabit some of the islands to the east and north of the eastern end of New Guinea. The communities form what might be called an "exchange ring" around which various kinds of articles are constantly passing from person to person in opposite directions, necklaces moving clockwise and arm bands counterclockwise. The Kula is an institution which embraces many activities and commands much of the interest of the communities which practice it.

The Kapauko in the Central Highlands of West New Guinea based their leadership on their networking relations with others within their own clan and tribe and with other clans. The society (social, economic, and political relations) depended on a system of debts and credits, and on being informed about what is going on socially and economically. The more important ones among them had contacts with leaders in other tribes in the highlands. Though there were no formal and regular contacts between the tribes north and south of the central highlands, apparently there were networks of contacts; flying over the uninhabited highland plains one will observe a network of footpaths, implying that there must be frequent contacts between tribes living in the mountain valleys and the coastal tribes (Poposil, 1954; Dubbeldam, 1964).

In another recent example, my son returned to our village from a term with a Dutch company in Africa. He bought a house, which demanded a lot of changes given the composition of his family. Partly the work was done by a contractor. Yet most of the work was done by himself and his friends—electricians, plumbers, and so on—who without any hesitance helped him, bringing in their own specific expertise and time. This is a network of young people who have known each other for many years, who not only sometimes play soccer or drink beer, but also help each other whenever needed.

CHARACTERISTICS

Benefits

Essential to a proper functioning of networks is the participants' belief that they have something worth sharing (see Namuddu in this book) and that they may call upon the others in the network when a need arises. This implies that in some cases one may find a two-way street, in other cases there may be a complex of one-way streets. The individual relation counts, as well as the total of relations.

Partnership

The partners in the network may be people or institutions with the same field of interest. Yet they may be in other disciplines or have other expertise, with a complementary effect. One must keep in mind that any individual or institution can be part of more than one network. This multidimensional aspect may be a strong asset to networking.

There is a difference between individual and institutional networks. It seems that individual networks depend more on personal characteristics and needs, rarely well defined, while institutional networks often are maintained because of well-defined interests. In practice there is a mix of the two.

Networking is an instrument of social communication and therefore it will reflect the participants' cultures. As a consequence the manners used in networking will be different in various cultures or between people of different cultures, such as, in an international network.

Partners in a network are often peers. However, people at different hierarchical levels can easily be partners in a network. The type of information or contribution given can be similar or different. In his inaugural address at the University of Utrecht, Kruijt discussed the important role of networking in the informal sector, giving examples from Latin America.

This characterization of how networking works is culturally bound. In most Western societies,

> networking is built upon simple calculations of benefits and costs. In the realm of non-confidential data and information, and as far as individual members of the network are not obliged to comply with collective wills, networking is usually perceived positively. In this sense, members in a network are seen as equals. This is less the case in East Asia. In China, Korea, or Japan, people exist in a hierarchy. Networking is therefore much easier achieved through official channels rather than through individuals. Members may comfortably interact with one another within recognized relations, while relations outside the official framework are less comfortable and indeed rare. . . . There are collaborations and communications between institutions, but very much along the official organizational lines. Networking in the Western sense of equal sharing and individuals joining freely, is not the norm. Cross-national networking, therefore, is even rarer. (Cheng, 1993, p. 13; see also his chapter in this book)

Objectives

This leads us to the issue of the objectives of networking. There is one major point, as Gmelin (1993) states "To be successful and viable there must be a strong self-interest for all participants in the network" (p. 13). The objectives of individual networking are normally less well-defined than those of institutional networking. The latter participate in a network because of their own institutional objectives:

- The Latin American Network of Education and Work is designed as a mechanism to exchange information that can lead to better utilization of research results (Gallart, 1993)
- European Network for Research on Learning and Instruction (EARLI) was established in 1985 "to *promote* the systematic exchange and discussion of ideas within the domain of instructional and educational research, as well as research on industrial training" (Entwistle, 1993, p. 24).

Here is an essential difference between individual and institutional networking. Gmelin (1993) writes: "Networks have to be mandated. The objectives of the network have to be correctly identified and activities have to be carefully planned" (p. 13).

This may be true for networks of institutions, especially when they have to consider the costs of participation in terms of priorities. It seems to be different for individuals, who often participate in networks because of an inner urge for communication or specific needs for information or support. This is especially the case for individuals within institutions who are cut off from communicative networks or for individuals who have a specific interest in something that does not fall within the mandate of their institution. Few academics or researchers in international education in the United Kingdom operate from large professional bases (Watson, 1993). The same seems to be true in many other countries. Participating in networks then is done out of necessity if one does not want to be cut off from academic brotherhood, information, and projects. As long as such individuals participate in a small network there is virtually no need for well-formulated objectives, and the activities of the network are neither mandated nor planned.

The reasons why people participate in networks are diverse. There is the need for information and the need for support and cooperation in any one of the participants' functions: teaching, research, and consultancy. By belonging to a wider group one has access to ideas and resources that make it possible to handle difficult situations (see Carton, "From Group to Network" in this book).

Formal and Informal

Informal networks are often characterized by a low frequency of formal meetings where all participants are present and low cost, and there is rarely a coordinating center of the network.

There are other cases when individuals or institutions participate in a formal network. For example, persons or institutions subscribe for membership or are part of the network as a result of an administrative agreement of their mandate. In this case one may question whether one should speak of networks or associations or similar formal institutions. In practice there seems to be a mix of the two. What one sees is that organizations participate in formal networks. Yet, the nature and the success of it depends strongly on the informal relations between the individuals in the participating organizations.

Though the basis for the network is a formal administrative structure, the citation suggests that the success of its operations depends much on informal networking between individuals.

Focal Point

In smaller networks all participants will likely know each other and be in touch with each other at one time or another. The larger a network becomes, the less people will know each other. There grows a need for other means of communication between the members, such as newsletters, mailings, or formal meetings. There is a fair chance that such a network will evolve into a formal association.

While still a small, informal network, some spontaneous members may take the initiative and stimulate the flow of communication so that the whole network keeps vibrating. As the network grows, or if it starts particular activities such as newsletters, projects, training, or the organization of formal meetings, the need arises for a focal point where activities can be coordinated and organized. More and more information will flow via this focal point.

Free Flow of Information

Exchange of information is one of the most important activities of networks. There are however various factors that hamper a free flow of information. To start with, some, perhaps many, people are hesitant to give away information or data from their own research or data collections for fear of competition. Scientists often are reluctant to give away information before they have published some final results. Furthermore there are political, economic, or social reasons why communication lines are partially or completely blocked.

Namuddu points at the absence of locally initiated and sustained communication as being in itself the most important evidence that the necessary community structure and beliefs needed to support functional networks have yet to emerge within Africa. Further development is needed in the process of democratization to allow flows of information; so far only a small segment of society is involved in genuine democratization. Furthermore, the few existing functional networks are still donor driven. As a consequence of this dependency, their participants have not yet managed to create a locally supported rationale for their existence, including the development of democratic mechanisms for expanding the networks within particular countries.

During a recent meeting on Education for All held in Warchau one sensed the need felt by teachers for new opportunities for the exchange of information through networks (meetings, seminars, etc.) outside existing teachers' organizations and unions, and for training programs that prepare teachers for new roles in a market economy. An essential part of the democratization process seems to be the search for information and the exchange of ideas and experiences.

Equipment

More and more networking is dependent on equipment and other means in order to communicate with the other participants. One may think of postal services, telephone, telex, telefax, e-mail, road and air transport, seminars, conferences, newsletters, journals, and databanks. Networking is no longer simply visiting other participants in the network.

In many places such means of communication are lacking or, if they are available, they function poorly and use is expensive. Someone has to pay the bill. Budgetary constraints make it more and more difficult for focal points to provide communication services for the networks for free. The costs of communication lead to dependency on donor agencies or sponsors. Some of these assist individuals to attend meetings, others are willing to support newsletters. There are occasional grants for building up documentation systems.

One may conclude that donors have difficulties in supporting networks. Somehow networks are not concrete enough; they are too elusive. Supporting institutions, training programs, teaching materials, and similar activities are much more attractive because there are visible and concrete results.

Institution Building

Lauglo has a hunch that those activities which are launched as network projects tend to be transitory. The projects are only a short-term, intensive stage toward getting something else done. He may be right to some extent when networks are launched as projects. But not all networks are launched. Many just grow from contacts between a few individuals. Others feel that they may profit from sharing information and ideas with them and join them, and after a while there is something we call a network. One may question whether such people really have concrete objectives in mind that must lead to something else. It seems also that many networks never do lead to something else, the participants may change gradually, maybe the focus of interest, but it is never institutionalized.

Yet practice shows that many networks just end up as something else. In the late 1950s, there were some scholars, people belonging to nongovernmental organizations, and people from quite different disciplines, who were concerned about the development of education in the countries in the Third World which were gaining independence one by one. They met, discussed, and published. Only later they felt that they had to do something concrete, namely to found a center that could carry out research and in this way be instrumental in helping to improve the educational situation. So the Centre for the Study of Education in Developing Countries (CESO) was founded.

In the 1970s, there were some young scholars in different fields interested in education in developing countries, who met each other in smaller or larger groups of differing composition, exchanged information, taught, and published. Somehow CESO became the focal point for this group, with only very small financial inputs (paying for the coffees and teas and offering an opportunity to disseminate ideas and experience in low-cost publications, such as the CESO *Verhandelingen*). Then they decided that together they could organize a module in education in developing countries at one of the universities. This started in the mid-1970s, when the Institute of Cultural Anthropology of the University offered hospitality and the course has continued until today. Participants in the network still contribute to the lecture series. But then, finally, since there were problems with credits for those who completed the course and because there were no opportunities to continue at postgraduate level, it was proposed to install a chair in education in developing countries at the University of Utrecht.

In both cases the participants in the networks definitely did not have a particular concrete goal or some institutionalized form in mind. Yet, both ended up in some institution. The participants still meet as partners in a quiet, informal network as a focal point serviced by CESO on a low-cost budget.

Networking can be instrumental in institution building. It is a mistake, however, to use networking as a cheap alternative for the costs, procedures, and time involved in institution building. It can be helpful for institution building if it is part of the process and additional to other instruments.

It is not always clear what is meant by donors when networking is the nature of a project. A year ago, it appears, the European Community (EC) started a program of networking between a large number of institutions in the Mediterranean and institutions in the member states. The question is whether this really is networking or just a system in which particular activities like fellowships, attachments, seminars, and research can be financed.[1] Networking in this context clearly is instrumental for institution building.

The value of networking in institution building may be illustrated by another example. In the 1970s, the Indonesian Linguistic Development Project (ILDEP) was started by the Netherlands Development Cooperation. One of the major objectives of this project was to provide the Indonesian National Centre for Linguistic Development (NCLD) with a professional staff of linguists who were well trained and qualified to teach, do research, and solve problems. Other objectives included the improvement of the administrative and organizational capacity of the center and the improvement of the library, the documentation facilities, and the technical equipment in view of its training function. It meant training 150 language researchers in a step-by-step program lasting, for those who reached the end, six years. There was a sequential mix of workshops, training, seminars, research, language training, and, for those who excelled, doctorate studies in the Netherlands and in Indonesia. Participants came from the NCLD, universities, and government institutions. Those who dropped out after a step still got something out of their training. The program resulted in a large number of publications and former participants got a feel for doing research. It is interesting that the participants got a sense of belonging to the network of linguists in Indonesia. Furthermore, the Dutch partner connected the project, or rather the participants in the programs, with its linguistic networks in the region and Europe. As a result, the product of the program is not only institution building and numbers of trained professionals, but also the introduction of Indonesian linguists into national and international networks, which in turn proved very stimulating for institution building.

Lauglo's hunch may be partly correct. If networking, and especially its spirit, is used in addition to other activities, it can be a very useful instrument in institution building, as long as the habit of networking is maintained.

NOTE

1. The information available when writing this chapter is rather flimsy. It may be worthwhile to explore how the system actually functions.

NETWORKING
AS A KNOWLEDGE SYSTEM

Kenneth King

Apart from the traditional and more recent systems for accessing existing knowledge (libraries, bibliographies, databases, etc.), networking has emerged as a supplementary or almost an alternative way of generating information. Networking emphasizes that the information is embedded in people, particular people, and that the quality of the personal connections to information will differ from other forms of data acquisition. What keeps the lecture and tutorial systems going, even in the most data-rich societies, must be some element of the additional value expected from personal contact. An element of the same principle operates in networking; at its most basic the search for knowledge via a network emphasizes that personal ties and obligations to share knowledge will produce information not easily found through alternative methods.

Examples would include the search for candidates for a job or a major task, where it may often be the case that while the job is officially and formally advertised via the media, candidates are also sought via a personal network of communication. Thus academics may put their names on databases of consultants but are aware that the personal phone call around a small network is the quickest way for an agency to decide who is available. For policy makers wanting someone immediately for a consultancy or wanting information about what's worth reading, the traditional search through consultant files or databases, even when computerized, may not be nearly so quick as three or four phone calls to people who are themselves at the center of one or more networks.

Information derived from databases, whether about individuals or about themes and issues in the literature, does not make value judgments about the persons concerned or the quality of the article, report, or book. The consultant database will not reveal whether the individual is a good colleague or team member or whether the article is really state of the art. For a busy decision maker, access to a database that will provide twenty abstracts from different journals about class size or about quality issues in vocational training is really of little help. For the policy maker who is prepared to read anything at all, the database will not say that one single piece on that topic is better than the other nineteen put together. Nor will it say that a particular person evident in the database and the literature search is persistently late in finishing contracts, projects, or reports. But this is what policy makers require.

So, personal networks of mutual obligation may be used widely to gain additional qualitative comments on people and on literature, including commentary on the attitudes and values of particular individuals. These informal networks operate everywhere. The question is whether formal networks which individuals may join on their own initiative are likely to offer some of the added value that is associated with the personal circle. A lot will depend on the scale and size of the network. And a lot will depend on whether the sense of personal obligation that fuels informal circles can be transferred to a more formal network. With the move from a circle or a club to a network, is it possible to maintain a culture of interdependence and obligation?

KNOWLEDGE AS A GUARDED SCARCE COMMODITY VERSUS KNOWLEDGE AS ABUNDANT AND SHARED

Databases with their immediate access, synthesizing, and abstracting potential across entire fields of research emphasize that in the public domain the search for information has been dramatically speeded up, provided the searcher is in an environment with access to computers, phone lines, and so on. There remains a tension, however, between knowledge retention and knowledge dissemination. Early access to privileged knowledge may give a comparative advantage for a researcher to get a consultancy, win a contract or whatever. If interinstitutional and interindividual competition is a feature of academic life and exists in a different form in aid agencies and nongovernmental organizations (NGOs), what catalyzes a network to share information? What is the advantage of democratizing access to scarce knowledge if knowledge is a form of investment capital? Why make more public what may be of private benefit?

Information in a network newsletter or bulletin is obviously different from a major article in a refereed journal which is public but trademarked and copyrighted by an individual or team. Often material in a network newsletter does not even fall into the category of a scarce commodity, as the more valued goods are traded via the association's journal. The situation is clearly different in networks whose newsletter is one of their principal products.

One reason for expanding access to scarce information is advocacy: the desire to involve a larger number of people in knowing about a particular policy, and to seek to influence it. To be effective, advocacy has to be rapid, and it usually cannot be dependent on the regular timing of a bulletin or journal.

Another reason for opening access to scarce information is that a lot of the key meetings and activities related to the analysis of policy for education and training in developing countries are by invitation only. If a network is concerned with the analysis and improvement of education policy in the North as a means to support education and training in the South, then it becomes essential to map and track major developments in policy formulation in the North. Sharing relevant information across the North, and from North to South and vice versa, is one way to do this.

A further dimension of the trade in information may be seen as taking place within the network itself. An individual member will be prepared to put some substantive information into the network (to other individuals directly or to the bulletin) if that person sees that the bulletin and the network act as a market place. If this trade in information about education and development is to be successful and sustainable, then the majority of members of the network need to be both buying and selling—acquiring information from the network and putting information back in for the benefit of others. These metaphors from trade and from markets may not be ideal but they are intended to underline the reciprocity and symmetry that ideally should exist if a network is to avoid becoming the voice of its coordinator and bulletin editor.

THE GLOBAL CHALLENGE OF NETWORKING

Depending on what the content and purpose of the network are, there are powerful pressures to ensure that the network has a multinational range. A network that has taken as one of its objectives the critical review of research on policies and strategies in the North that have implications for the South requires a network that spans the countries where policy is developed and has some outreach to countries where aid policy has impact. The essential issue is that the network reflect the character of the task it has undertaken.

It can be seen from the networks mentioned in this book (see Appendix 3) that there is a multiplicity of network connections in education and training that straddle the North and the South. Some are subject specific, such as science and technology education and adult education; some are based on professional associations such as the World Council of Comparative Education Societies (WCCES); and others are primarily regional but have implications for other regions, such as the Red Latinoamericana de Información y Documentación en Educación (RE-DUC).

Some of the following more fundamental questions need to be addressed: What would the ideal shape of North-South relations in education and training be like? What would be the character of an improved aid relationship: less aid? more aid? aid-free zones? Can any substantial shift be expected in the current Northern dominance of the discourse on Southern educational requirements?

NETWORKING BETWEEN RESEARCHERS AND POLICY MAKERS

Noel F. McGinn

The process of communication is essential to networking, a fancy word for the construction and use of relatively stable patterns of communication. There are at least three points of view about the communication canyon that separates researchers and policy makers. One perspective argues that policy makers lack the preparation necessary to understand research reports. The task is to change the receiver. Miller's (1983) review of use of research in the Caribbean seemed to support this view. Reforms recommended by research were more likely to be made public policy when the study authors were called into public service. Pursuing this vision, assistance agencies increase funding to provide policy makers with training in research, first in the social sciences, more recently in economics. Researchers intensify their efforts to develop statistical techniques to support their claims of causality. Policy analysis provides clear directions for policy makers to follow.

A second point of view is that researchers lack an understanding of policy per se and the political process in which decisions are made. From this perspective, the task is to change the sender. Most of the proponents of this perspective are doubtful about whether the dominant approach to research can, in fact, supply answers to the kinds of questions that policy makers have to answer. The doubts are about research that assumes that problems and answers merely swirl about in history waiting for someone to discover them. The most critical task in changing reality is first to understand why it should be changed.[1] Researchers are trained to be more effective consultants, that is, to assist their clients in clarification of their objectives. This perspective implicitly assumes that truth speaks to power, that is, that once goals have been defined, the researcher can indicate which actions should be taken.

The third perspective argues that policies will be most effective when policy makers, researchers, and other participants, develop a shared consensus about what it is that should be done and how best to go about it. The differences in understanding and values of researchers and policy makers are legitimate and should be acknowledged as the basis for negotiating a common understanding of a reality yet to be created. Truth and power are not fixed quantities. Research and policy are linked dialectically; each changes the other in dynamic ways, so that outcomes are governed by emergent probabilities, that is, they often are unpredictable. Policy analysis can be effective for indicating the possible consequences of alternative actions, but it cannot indicate which alternative should be chosen.

COMMUNICATION AND CULTURE

Communication over a sustained period of time affects participants. To be able to communicate effectively, participants have to share language. This sharing has to take place not just at an objective or denotative level (when I say "chair" I mean an object with three or four legs on which you can sit), but also at a subjective or connotative level (chairs are used by educated people, others sit on the ground; a gentleman offers a lady a chair; the chair person should be respected). Language shapes the way we think and colors the meanings we give to things. We socialize children, for example, through the language we encourage them to use, specifying what words can be used in what circumstances. The effect of communication is dialectical: we are more likely to communicate with people who are like us, that is, share a language, but communication also makes us more alike.

The meanings that a group of people share are an important part of what is called culture, those patterned forms of behavior and systems of values that distinguish one group of people from another. When we talk about the culture of an organization, we refer not just to the peculiar behaviors at the annual picnic, but also to the shared meanings of the members. These are reflected in the signs and symbols used within the organization, in patterns of communication, and in special terminologies. If members of the organization communicated only with each other over time (perhaps several generations) they would develop a unique language that would not be understandable by nonmembers.

Not all forms of communication are equally effective in generating culture, however. Sender-driven communication makes few contributions. Changes are limited, as the sender's concern is for receipt of specific messages. Sender and receiver continue to be clearly distinguished from each other.

The use of a strictly receiver-oriented approach to communication also fails to generate shared values and meanings that persist over time. For instance, some cynical consultants may easily slip on and off the cultural dress of their clients, but novice consultants are trained to keep clear the distinction between themselves and their clients.

SOME CONDITIONS THAT LIMIT DEVELOPMENT AND MAINTENANCE OF THE CULTURE OF ORGANIZATIONS

As organizations grow in size, the time required for all members to communicate with each other (thereby maintaining the organization's culture) increases geometrically. In addition, a longer time elapses between the definition of objectives and the methods to achieve them, and the observation of the effects of those methods when applied. This makes organizational consensus and coherence more difficult to maintain.

The maintenance of organizational culture also is more difficult in organizations concerned with issues that affect only a small proportion of their members' lives. These are known as secondary organizations; they draw members from a spectrum of primary organizations that have wider claims on members' time and values. The more varied the membership of the secondary organization, the more work has to be done to achieve a common language with shared meanings. Primary and secondary are of course relative terms. A given organization may draw members from other secondary or even tertiary organizations. This complicates the process of developing an organizational culture.

Finally, it is more difficult to develop and maintain the culture of an organization when the organization's purpose is effective communication with other organizations. This communication with other organizations can weaken ties to the first. When the other organizations change, the first organization may have to adjust its own goals and means in order to maintain its networks. Rapid changes in the other organizations can severely strain the internal coherence of the first organization.

A Hierarchical Solution to the Problem of Maintaining Organizational Coherence

One way to achieve and maintain shared understandings is to establish a hierarchy of authority that monitors and controls values of members of the organization and which resists pressures for change from other organizations. Organizations that pursue this strategy draw sharp boundaries between goal setting, policy analysis, and implementation, and between the persons responsible for them. Top policy makers may see their organization as secondary to another in which they are primary members. They communicate laterally with their counterparts in other organizations for the definition of values, and then downward to their subordinates responsible for administration and operations.

Subordinates, on the other hand, are required to define the organization as primary. Coherence is maintained by careful recruitment and selection of persons who already share the organization's values, and by careful socialization of new members. Communications from policy makers about organizational values use a sender-driven approach. Subordinates are encouraged to network actively among themselves for the development of shared (and organizationally sanctioned) values. On those few occasions in which subordinates communicate with other organizations, they are encouraged to use a sender-driven approach.

In hierarchical organizations, policy making is a process of discovering which means are most effective for achieving goals set by policy makers. Discovery is accomplished by experts in the use of methods of objective science. Facts are taken as universal, and therefore can be validated by means of replication in time and space. Networking among the experts (sometimes called policy analysts) confirms the discoveries' validity. The policy analysts speak truth to power (at the policy level), but claim they do not exercise power themselves, for to do so would be to jeopardize their objectivity.

Implementation of policy is the responsibility of a third group. It is seen as a technical task that can be carried out correctly only if it is not adulterated by politics or by the ignorance of implementors of goals and means. Persons at the operational level have to be informed, but they neither engage in subjective goal setting nor in objective discovery of the truth.

In practice policy analysts often feel obliged to attempt to influence decisions of policy makers. They justify their action by reference to policy makers' ignorance of the facts and reliance on subjective thinking. There are at least four means by which policy analysts influence the policy debate: (1) using technical jargon and sophisticated analyses that others cannot critique; (2) appealing to openness and dependence on experts; (3) arguing that a political issue is actually a technical issue; and (4) holding back information about other alternatives, misrepresenting the validity of analyses, and claiming success for untested options (Forrester, 1988).

When analysts work with other organizations, they may engage in policy dialogue, defined as

> a process of *marketing*, as opposed to *design*, of the policy reform. To put it crudely, it is a highly sophisticated, carefully crafted sales job that creates the feeling of inclusiveness and co-ownership of the reform process. The best situation is if such a process in fact *is* inclusive and is in fact co-owned by all the stake-holders, as long as the consultative nature does not extend to the basic choices but creates ownership of the decisions after the fact. (Crouch, 1993, p. 10)[2]

The dialogue is organized with presentation of "objective" facts produced by unassailable statistical analyses. A major champion of this approach argues that to the extent that we stick to the facts we can avoid the introduction of any "ism" which distorts our understanding and leads us away from effective action. Reasonable people will agree on what the critical issues are and careful research will indicate the correct responses (Psacharopoulos, 1990). The effect is to inhibit "subjective" thought of politicians and implementors. They are helped to achieve clarity by technical arguments couched in language they do not understand, but with the bottom line clearly drawn. In these instances, networking is principally a means to communicate "correct" information.

A Nonhierarchical Approach to the Problem of Consensus

In nonhierarchical (and sometimes heterarchical) organizations, or in those that include members with highly diverse interests, the problem of definition of goals for the organization can only be resolved by developing a consensus among their members, that is, by members coming to agree with each other on those activities they will carry out in common. This is most likely the more members of the organization participate in mutual definition of goals, and definition of means to attain them. This requires the construction of a shared view of reality, which comes about through sustained conversation among the members.

In this communication, subjective facts are not only legitimate but have greater importance than objective facts, especially for the definition of goals. Policy, in this kind of process, becomes what everyone in the organization understands they want to do in order to achieve shared objectives. Networking is the instrument for continuous re-examination of ends and means, and the iterative building of a shared perception of reality. The reality in question includes both of what are commonly called value and fact. Policy making is then a process of generating consensus among members of the organization about what is desired and how best to achieve it. There are no experts, except perhaps in the generation of the process.

As suggested above, this approach to development of coherence through consensus generation produces contradictions within secondary organizations. The culture of the secondary organization that develops high consensus can begin to take precedence over the culture of the primary organization from which the members are drawn. If communication with other organizations follows a sender-driven or a consultancy model, the problem can be intensified. Especially if the secondary organization controls resources sought by others, it can develop autonomy with respect to the primary organizations of its members and its clients. This is the basis for our complaints about bureaucratic organizations: they forget why they were created.

IMPLICATIONS

Each of these two kinds of organizations has a culture consistent with and defined by the processes of policy making. The culture of the hierarchical organization is highly specified, relatively comprehensive, and exclusive. Members know exactly what is expected of them, and the norms and rules cover many aspects of their lives. The organization's success in dealing with a complex and turbulent environment depends on its ability to generate or mobilize enough energy to impose its perspective on others in the environment, preferably through persuasion. According to one proponent, "The task of the policy support layer is to provide the high-level technocratic nucleus with the data, analysis, and marketing tools to crush the special interest groups in the public debate arena" (Crouch, 1993, p. 8).[3]

The nonhierarchical organization draws its boundaries more widely. Its success in dealing with a complex and turbulent environment depends on its ability to include within its culture (its shared meanings, norms, values, and behaviors) groups that may be highly divergent on other characteristics, yet share values with respect to the mission of the organization. As a consequence, the culture is not as well defined nor as comprehensive. Nonhierarchical organizations face the problem of how to generate enough internal consensus to have any energy to influence their environment, or even their membership.

Inclusive organizations, those that draw their members from many primary organizations, suffer a lack of definition and can fail to generate enough energy to make any positive contributions. Networking is the solution, as a means to develop a common culture, that will permit the organization to speak with a single voice and mobilize resources to make contributions.

This is more likely to occur if networking is both extensive, covering all members, and intensive, covering more than just objective facts about education and development. Only if networking approaches what might be called intimate conversation can we begin to develop a shared understanding of the problems that need to be addressed, and the ways to address them. Limitation of networking to a policy dialogue that seeks to validate objective facts about education and development will leave a weak organization that lacks definition.

One of the conditions that will limit intensive networking is heterogeneity of cultures. The cultures from which an organization draws its membership have different norms about how much intimacy is allowed between persons from different groups (gender, ethnic, social, etc.). Part of the networking task will be to discover forms of intimacy that are mutually acceptable.

A second condition is physical distance. Intimacy requires closeness. An organization with members in several continents who infrequently see each other will have to work harder to achieve consensus and coherence. The challenge is to use networking to include a wider variety of perspectives while increasing intimacy, or to push hard for internal coherence and cohesion while avoiding distancing ourselves from the groups we wish to serve. The resolution of these contradictions will require a good deal of self-consciousness by an organization.

NOTES

1. This is the point of view of Argyris (1980). He argues that in order to meet the methodological requirements of objectivist social science we have to distance ourselves from human actors, making it unlikely that we will have a good understanding of what is going on.

2. Crouch is recommending this approach as a means for donors to have impact on policy reforms. See also Crouch, Vegas, and Johnson (1993).

3. Special interest groups are those who oppose the public interest as defined by the policy analysts.

SPECIALIST NEWSLETTERS AND NETWORKS

Kenneth King

One way or another the newsletter plays an essential part in networking. The newsletter sometimes seeks to make the membership of a professional association (with an academic journal) feel more in touch. The long lead time of the journal contrasts with what can be the very short lead times of a newsletter. Newsletters suggest bottom-up mechanisms with their emphasis on news from the regions and news from correspondents, but often this communication must be stimulated by pleas from the editor. This chapter describes an incomplete variety of newsletters, to illustrate how they may serve readers' interests.

BASIC EDUCATION–INNOVATIONS NETWORKS

The *Forum for Advancing Basic Education and Literacy* started in 1991, and emerged from the Basic Research and Implementation in Developing Education Systems Project (BRIDGES) Forum that had knit together project sites participating in that United States Agency for International Development (USAID) project. In its new format (between twelve and sixteen pages, with color) it seeks to "report on research and inventive and innovative programs that address some of the obstacles to achieving universal access to and completion of primary education." In this sense it is a post-Jomtien newsletter,[1] but its aim is to reach policy makers with the latest advances in education worldwide; more specifically, the latest advances and innovations in basic education. In one way, the *Forum* can be conceptualized within the history of the innovations networks set up by the United Nations Educational, Scientific, and Cultural Organization (UNESCO) many years back. It has its feature on "Innovators in Education," for example. But its particular angle has to be coming up with enough copy on suggestive innovations in basic education to hold the readership and the support of the funding body.

ABEL Information Bulletin: Advancing Basic Education and Literacy is closely connected to the previous one. The *Forum* was operated by the Harvard Institute for International Development (HIID) in collaboration with the Academy for Educational Development (AED), Creative Associates International (CAI), and the Research Triangle Institute (RTI), while the *Bulletin* is operated by AED in association with the other three. *ABEL Information Bulletin* has a somewhat different flavor. Its aim seems to be to transfer into the hands of the policy community "practical and relevant information about basic education initiatives and innovations in basic education reform."

What makes it particularly pithy is its attempt to communicate and disseminate what it calls "proven tools, methods, and research findings about basic education programs." Many of these short bulletins are just a few pages outlining the context, the problem, the methods, and then the lessons learned. As of June 1992 there were thirty-six *Bulletins*.

What is interesting about this strong emphasis on innovation is that it is not restricted to these sister network bulletins. There has for years been a bulletin from the International Bureau of Education (IBE), currently called *Education Innovation and Information*. (It has reached number seventy-two, which is some achievement for a bulletin/newsletter!) It does not seem to do now what I recall it doing in the earlier years, mentioning particular initiatives and innovations in education. The current issue has national and international news, viewpoint, regional news, and an "In Brief" column. But in the light of this existing bulletin and the existing innovations networks of UNESCO, it is intriguing to see that, emerging from Jomtien there is a major UNESCO project to promote innovations in basic education, under the title Education for All: Making it Work. The scheme aims to (1) improve basic education through innovations, (2) go to scale with promising innovations, and (3) bring about an active scheme of cooperation and experience exchange among developing countries. Again, possibly influenced by the round-tables in Jomtien, there is an emphasis on a video bank of innovations in basic education, currently holding some twenty-two videos.

There are other newsletter/network children of Jomtien. Emerging from the World Council on Education for All (WCEFA) *Bulletin*, there started, after Jomtien *EFA 2000*, a bulletin published by UNESCO as the lead agency for the official follow-up to the world conference. A second clear child of Jomtien is *Education News: The Newsletter of the UNICEF Education Cluster*. Unlike *EFA 2000*, this is really a vehicle for communication between headquarters and the field offices.

NETWORKING ADULT EDUCATION AND LITERACY

With a number of new newsletters in the post–Jomtien era, we mustn't forget the old newsletters. Several of them have been working for a long time on the adult and adult literacy side of basic education. Notable among these are *UNESCO Adult Education: Information Notes*, which itself surveys many of the other newsletters and bulletins relating to adult education and literacy. Another of the established newsletters relating to adult education is *ICAE NEWS: Newsletter of the International Council for Adult Education* (ICAE). ICAE is itself a major international NGO which claims, as of 1992, to comprise ninety-two national, regional, and sectoral member associations, involving seventy-four countries. And then there is the UNESCO Institute of Education *UIE Newsletter*. The UIE has itself been dedicated to the analysis of literacy for many years, and through the *Newsletter* it is possible to find out about the Literacy Exchange Network in both the industrialized countries and its parallel in the developing countries. For each there is a directory of members. Finally, a more recent example of the established newsletters is *CAETA Newsletter,* for which the Commonwealth Association for the Education and Training of Adults (CAETA) is responsible.

EDUCATIONAL TECHNOLOGIES, AND SCIENCE AND TECHNOLOGY EDUCATION

Another set of networks relate to learning technologies. For many years, USAID has supported research on learning technologies, but Jomtien has helped to focus the importance of lessons learned in many different projects. These lessons learned are available in "Fact Sheets" from *LearnTech Forum: Learning Technologies for Basic Education.* And LearnTech, which is coordinated by the Education Development Centre, is in turn in touch with a consortium of North and South American members. The new newsletter (volume 1, number 1, 1991) acts as a link among consortium members. Separate from the educational technologies associated with LearnTech are the newsletters concerned with science and technology education. Here, the British Council's *Science Education Newsletter* (now issue number 102) is a very valuable way of keeping in touch, both about activities in the United Kingdom and overseas and international activities.

A relatively recent useful newsletter would include *ComLearn: News Publication of the Commonwealth of Learning.* This had reached just volume 3 in 1992, reflecting the recent arrival of COL. Through the newsletter, not surprisingly, it is possible to glimpse the wider network of which COL is a new member, including the International Council for Distance Education (ICDE). Another newsletter reflecting on higher education is *WHE News* (Worldwide Higher Education News) produced by the British Council's Higher Education Group.

Within the European Community alone there are a whole series of newsletters, many of them concerned with education and youth policy, of which perhaps just the most recent is *Education & Training* whose first issue was in June 1991.

REFLECTIONS ON NEWSLETTER NETWORKING

Many newsletters are available only as one of several advantages of belonging to a professional association. Thus the very useful newsletters of several of the comparative education societies (for instance, in the United Kingdom, the United States, France, Canada, and most recently South Africa) tend only to be received if the interested person has already joined the relevant society and thus gets the society's professional academic journal. In some cases, like the United Kingdom, the news-letter can be acquired by becoming an associate member of the professional society.

Second, not all newsletters have a network function, as well as a dissemination function. For many, one of the most interesting things to know about newsletters would be the size of the mailing list and how it is kept up to date. It also would be valuable to know how membership or circulation is divided between industrialized and developing countries.

A third value of newsletters has to be their commentary on publications, conferences, and activities. Some of this may prove frustrating, as library policies may prevent acquisition of new journals, and many of the more interesting events may require membership. But a very great deal of what can be discovered in newsletters can feed into teaching, research, and so on. The problem perhaps for most people receiving newsletters is having the time to read them in order to act on the news that has become available. How many of us keep newsletters on the shelf, waiting for time to read them at leisure, and then find that the material is two years old when finally time has been found!

NOTE

1. In 1990, ministers of education from 150 countries, officials of bilateral and multilateral assistance agencies, and education researchers met in Jomtien, Thailand to discuss how to extend basic education to all children.

TRANSREGIONAL NETWORKS

PART II

Included in this section are three examples of networks intended to link persons and institutions across regions. UNESCO has perhaps the longest experience and greatest variety of experiences of any group concerned with communication between different groups about education. In addition to networks in five regions of the world, there are also central efforts to insure a high level of flow of information. A major vehicle for this is the International Bureau of Education (IBE) in Geneva, which serves as a center of documentation for education information generated around the world, but also has a major responsibility for dissemination.

A second example is the work of the Commonwealth Secretariat, coordinating activities and communication among the United Kingdom and former colonies. There is an explicit concern for networking to link professionals together across national boundaries. This is pursued through a variety of approaches, at the level of higher education, technical training, training of school administrators, attention to special issues affecting women, the small states, and so on.

The United Nations Children's Fund's (UNICEF) contribution is a network of professionals concerned with early childhood care and development. Although the focus of concern is relatively narrow, this is a worldwide network which over time has produced a great amount of information. This brief piece provides useful information about how to make a network work and what to do when it is successful, or at least attracts members. As the network grows, the quality of exchanges among members can suffer. A newsletter that once was much like a chain letter among friends can become a more formalized publication of high technical quality, perhaps, but not necessarily serving well the interests of the network. (For newsletters, see Appendix 3.)

These three papers offer only a glimpse of the issues involved in transregional networking. They fail to provide a solid analysis of the effectiveness (at any moment and over time) of these ambitious endeavors. When still a small group, perhaps it is easy to know how well the network is doing. As it grows in size, however—when the group "graduates" to become a network—more formal methods of assessment may become necessary.

UNESCO NETWORKS IN EDUCATION AND TRAINING WORLDWIDE

Juan Carlos Tedesco

UNESCO operates different kinds of networks, according to its fields of activities and institutional frameworks. Even though priorities set up for their activities differ from one region to another, all networks are basically designed to promote cooperation and the exchange of innovative information, experience and expertise among member states. In the field of innovations in education, there are five regional networks:

1. Network of Educational Innovation for Development in Africa (NEIDA, Dakar)
2. Educational Innovation Programme for Development in the Arab States (EIPDAS, Kuwait)
3. Asia and Pacific Programme of Educational Innovation for Development (APEID, Bangkok)
4. Caribbean Network of Educational Innovation for Development (CARNEID, Bridgetown)
5. Programme of Cooperation in Research and Development for Educational Innovation in South and Southeast Europe (CODIESE)

UNESCO headquarters' principal function is to ensure the networks' smooth operation. Program priorities and modalities of implementation are determined through consultations among participating member states. All these networks exchange and disseminate both research findings and practical experience in the field of educational innovations.

The regional networks in education bear witness to UNESCO's decentralization policy of educational programs, the main aim of which is to understand better the realities of each region and achieve close cooperation with educational authorities of member states through regional cooperation. Global issues, and international and interregional cooperation are dealt with by headquarters, which also provides some technical and financial assistance to these networks.

In the field of information and documentation in education, the International Bureau of Education (IBE, Geneva) operates the International Network for Educational Information (INED), which cooperates with more than 100 focal points, designated by national authorities, in charge of national educational information networking and international contacts and exchange in the field of educational information. The IBE issues an *INED Newsletter* through which information is circulated; INED participants are invited to make their activities better known through INED "identity cards" attached to the newsletter in order to promote and encourage the exchange of information and documentation.

In addition, UNESCO has promoted and operates other networks in the framework of the major regional projects in basic education. In Latin America and the Caribbean region, for instance, UNESCO is operating specialized networks in the fields of

1. literacy (REDALF—Red de Alfabetización, regional network for training personnel and providing specific support for literacy and adult education programs),
2. quality of education and teacher training (PICPEMCE—Regional Network for Teacher Training),
3. management (REPLAD—Regional Network for the Planning and Administration of Literacy Development),
4. information (SIRI—Regional Information System).

The most specific and important aspect of these networks is the articulation between their different components: governmental and nongovernmental institutions as well as academic and political institutions. The dialogue and exchange of experiences, information, and approaches enables this kind of network to play a central role in the design and implementation of the Plan of Action for the major project of each planning period.

The success of UNESCO's networking activities in education depends on several factors, such as (1) the quality of the information provided by these networks, in terms of its relevance to the needs of users, (2) the usability and applicability of this information, particularly for educational decision making, (3) the high quality of communicability, in terms of the language and presentation used for its dissemination, (4) the networks' capacity to sustain, stimulate and develop cooperative attitudes and actions among their participants, (5) the networks' capacity to maintain both political will and specialists' continued intellectual contributions to their input, and (6) the networks' capacity to create stimulating projects and attract extra-budgetary funding for them.

The most important lesson learned by UNESCO's networks is that the sharing of experiences, processes, informal links, and problem-solving methods is of great importance, maybe even greater, than the mere sharing of information.

COMMONWEALTH NETWORKS IN EDUCATION

Education Team at the Commonwealth Secretariat

The Commonwealth provides a supportive context for links and networks in education reflecting features in terms of similar education traditions and structures, shared language, and a number of Commonwealth-wide and regional professional associations.

A new institution which links up many of the distance education institutions is the Commonwealth of Learning (COL) in Vancouver. The database at the International Center for Distance Learning at the Open University in Milton Keynes is Britain's contribution to COL. It constitutes a rich store of information on distance education institutions and programs, that is not confined to Commonwealth countries.

There are a number of well-established associations which bind Commonwealth education institutions together and provide a framework for joint activities and the sharing of experience and information. The longest established is undoubtedly the Association of Commonwealth Universities (ACU) based in London and having almost 400 subscribing institutions in its membership. Another institutional membership body is the Commonwealth Association of Polytechnics in Africa (CAPA), which was founded in 1978 and has over 130 technical and vocational institutions in its membership; its headquarters is in Nairobi.

Three professional associations in the education field are the Commonwealth Council for Educational Administration, founded in 1970 and headquartered in Australia; the Commonwealth Association of Science, Technology, and Mathematics Educators, founded in 1978 and its secretariat located in London; and the Commonwealth Association for the Education and Training of Adults, founded in the late 1980s and based at the University of Zimbabwe in Harare. These associations have several hundred individual members, publish newsletters, and organize seminars and conferences.

THE COMMONWEALTH SECRETARIAT AND EDUCATION NETWORKING

The Education Programme of the Commonwealth Secretariat (ComSec) sees as one of its main functions the promotion of professional linkages and networks among professionals in Commonwealth developing countries. In a number of different areas of work it has tried to build communities of professionals with shared concerns who meet together to address common problems and engage in joint activities such as training workshops or the cooperative production of re-source materials and handbooks.

The program is working with selected Commonwealth universities to establish a consortium to promote student flows from industrialized to developing countries, and between developing countries. It is envisaged that the proposed consortium will consist, in the first instance, of a limited number of about twenty Common-wealth universities, drawn from both industrialized and developing countries. Exchange programs may be set up either on the basis of bilateral agreements between pairs of universities, or multilaterally, with students going to one of a number of universities offering different opportunities.

Women Managers in Higher Education

An informal set of links has emerged between ACU- and ComSec-organized training workshops, for the purpose of preparing women for management positions in higher education. Structurally, the use of common trainers provided natural cross-institutional and cross-regional connections. There is increasing evidence of such associations being sustained through staff development activi-ties initiated by individuals from institutions within countries as well as across countries.

Education Development in Small States of the Commonwealth

For ten years the secretariat's Education Programme has undertaken work on educational development in small states. The premise on which this work is based is that smallness of scale provides distinctive challenges for education policy and practice. A crucial part of this work is the belief that small states can benefit from sharing experience and working together on a pan-Commonwealth basis, accepting the great diversity which exists politically, culturally, and economically. Putting people in touch with people, facilitating exchange, individually and at the institu-tional level, and developing materials and courses are all part of a process of sharing to inform national practice. There are no formal networks (although professional associations in the Caribbean and South Pacific have been assisted by the Common-wealth) but there does now exist a body of people in small states, with an interest in small states, from which there has grown a literature and a network of informal but practical links.

SCIENCE, TECHNOLOGY, AND MATH EDUCATION (STME)

The secretariat, together with its major partners such as UNESCO, the International Development Research Centre (IDRC), and the Swedish International Development Agency (SIDA), has organized a series of activities directed at such issues as the participation of women and girls in Science, Technology, and Math Education (STME), shortages of math and science teachers, lack of teaching materials in these subjects, and the teaching of science through the process approach. The focus is on the training of key primary school science teacher educators. Through these activities, the secretariat has established links and networks with many national and international organizations which usually give support to many of the workshops and seminars undertaken. Although the secretariat's main partner in this area is the Commonwealth Association of Science, Technology, and Mathematics Educators (CASTME), it has also had support from other organizations, such as the International Foundation for Science, the Commonwealth Association of Polytechnics in Africa, and the Association of African Universities. National and regional professional bodies have also been very active in many secretariat activities.

TRAINING TECHNICIANS IN EQUIPMENT MAINTENANCE AND REPAIR

At a recent Commonwealth Secretariat workshop held in Kenya Polytechnic, Nairobi, it was stressed that hands-on workshops organized for the regions, such as those organized by the International Foundation for Science, resulted in considerable benefits of networking and establishing contacts. Technicians from the region met each other for the first time, had the opportunity to discuss similar problems, and often found they had the same make of equipment. This may result in less isolation in exchange of technical information, spare parts, or even consumables. Participants agreed that clearly the logical outcome of such benefits is to set up a network of users. The role of networks was discussed using particular examples of Network of Users of Scientific Equipment in Southern Africa (NUSESA) and Network for Instruments of Development Maintenance and Repair (NIDMAR) in South East Asia.

TEACHER MANAGEMENT IN AFRICA

The teacher management project (personnel information records, personnel procedures, and head teacher training and support) relies on an extending network of professionals in ministries, agencies, NGOs, and institutions. It is an informal network, developed over a period of six years, maintained by a project officer in the Commonwealth Secretariat Education Programme. Most communication is from the center out to those in the network, but increasingly, because of the long-term nature of the teacher management program, the high degree of consistency in the activities offered, and improved communications in Africa, members of the network interact with one another. The teacher management project also cooperates with the Commonwealth Council for Educational Administration, disseminating information through it and using it to identify professionals and consultants. The Donors to African Education, through its task force, secretariat, and various working groups, particularly the Working Group on the Teaching Profession, which the Commonwealth Secretariat leads, has proved a vital linking network.

CONSULTATIVE GROUP ON EARLY CHILDHOOD CARE AND DEVELOPMENT

Robert Myers

The knowledge network of the Consultative Group on Early Childhood Care and Development now reaches out to approximately 1,200 institutions or individuals in more than 100 countries. An attempt is made to involve only those individuals who have a direct interest in programming for the improvement of early childhood development. A cross section of sectors and disciplines is actively sought so that information will spread through the different subnetworks.

The network is given life in two main ways, through mailings and by personal contacts. The principal vehicle for exchange of information is a bulletin called the *Coordinators' Notebook*, published two times each year. The *Notebook* is distributed free of charge at present. The *s'* in the title of the bulletin is intended to indicate that each person who receives the *Notebook* is a coordinator of his or her own network. Those who receive the bulletin are urged to copy and share it on their own networks so that there is a multiplier effect. Participants are asked to contribute items to the publication. Each publication or meeting that is being presented in the *Notebook* carries with it an address where direct contact can be made. Occasionally, network participants are asked for their opinions with respect to a particular topic, as part of the process of producing a focus article. In addition to the above, documents of general interest are mailed occasionally to network participants between issues of the *Notebook*.

The second basis for exchange of information occurs through personal contacts. The consultative group helps to organize at least two meetings each year. Members of the secretariat of the group also travel to participate in meetings and/or in relation to other projects carried out under the auspices of the consultative group. Through these personal contacts the network grows and is given life.

LESSONS LEARNED

First, as a network grows in size it is ever more difficult to stimulate real exchange. At the outset it was possible to write a personal note to each of the approximately 200 individuals who were part of the network. That is not possible when the mailing grows to 1,200.

To get around this problem, a core group of approximately 200 individuals has been selected for special attention. Communication and exchange (as opposed to simply sending out information) with this subgroup is much higher than for the group in general. With size come potential problems of cost as well. It is likely that there will have to be a charge for distribution of the *Notebook* in the future. Our intention is to restrict the charge for participation in the knowledge network to individuals and institutions that can afford to subscribe.

Second, slicker is not necessarily better. With improvements in the format and general appearance of the *Coordinators' Notebook*, there seems to be a greater tendency for people to want to hang on to their copy. It is put on the shelf and is not shared, defeating the idea of the *s*'.

Finally, personal contacts through individual correspondence, in meetings, and in the course of travel are essential to make a network come to life. For this reason, it is important in those cases where an institution is the participant to identify an appropriate person in the institution with whom to communicate.

NORRAG

PART III

The Northern Research Review and Advisory Group (NORRAG) is also a transregional network. It is given a section of its own here to feature information about its operation, because it is linked with a number of other networks in the regions themselves.

In some respects the history of NORRAG is a history of modern concern for use of research to inform education policy in developing countries. King dates the earliest proposals with respect to explicit transfers of information in the early 1970s. Prior to that time bilateral assistance agencies, foundations, and other NGOs in wealthy countries had provided support to poorer nations. The development ideology prior to the 1970s privileged investment in high-level human resources, so university enrollments in many countries grew much more rapidly than did those in basic education. But economic stagnation and accompanying political instability continued or worsened.

A new strategy was required, one based on a more solid understanding of conditions in the countries and the most effective means for expanding appropriate education given those conditions. This would require a capability to carry out research on education. It was assumed that the provision of research to policy makers would lead to more effective education policies and practices.

One of the outcomes of this enlightenment was the funding by the International Development Research Centre (IDRC) of Canada of a means to compile, generate, and disseminate research pertinent to education policies. From this sponsorship developed many of the networking activities described in the pages that follow.

King describes how the original emphasis on dissemination of research changed over time. An early advance was insistence on communication between researchers and policy makers. Those responsible for implementation of policy, called practitioners, were added later. There was concern for communication between North and South.[1] Work began with an assumption that a great deal of information already existed in the South. State-of-the-art reviews of research would be used to identify the range of options available, rather than to suggest universal remedies. Given an interest in expansion of the range of options available to policy makers, reviewers attempted to include all that was "known," even if publication did not meet the canons of rigorous social science. Because the network included researchers and policy makers the advisory function became a dialogue among equals, rather than a process of transfer of knowledge from researchers to policy makers.

NORRAG is one of the organizations that emerged from the original IDRC grant, and is the sponsor of this book. King, and Carton in the following piece, provide details on the operation of NORRAG as a network. A critical reading of their texts indicates a shift away from dissemination of what is known toward development of a shared understanding through dialogue. Research and information continue to play a central role as the vehicle and focus of the dialogue, but the purpose of the association is now less the production of research and more the production of shared understanding. How to accomplish this at great distance and across cultural boundaries remains a central challenge.

Carton offers four suggestive criteria or concepts to assess the condition of a network. First, networks can be more or less connected to other systems. Networks that intend to have effects outside their membership require connections to the outside. Second, networks vary in the number of connections among their members. The more connections within the network that each member has, the more effective is the network. Third, if McGinn is right in insisting that internal connectedness leads over time to greater ease of communication, then the ability of parts of a network to communicate without the formal mechanisms set up by the center are evidence of success. Finally, a network succeeds only if there are few "free riders" or "spectators." Especially if one sees a network as a means for generation of knowledge, and not just its transmission, then the activeness of the membership is critical.

NOTE

1. These terms are dated now, and should be read in historical context.

NETWORKING, ADVOCACY, AND ADVICE: AN HISTORICAL PERSPECTIVE

Kenneth King

The origins of the Northern Research Review and Advisory Group (NORRAG) can be traced to about 1986, but the origins of the concept of a group that would be concerned with research, review, and advice go back much earlier, perhaps at least ten years earlier, to 1974–75. They are inseparable from the entry of the International Development Research Centre (IDRC) of Canada into the donor community, as a new kind of bilateral donor concerned solely with research and anxious to make its mark in the several different fields where it had chosen to work. And, in turn, the IDRC's concerns with education policy were to some extent shaped by the mood of international donors at the very beginning of the 1970s.

In brief, the consensus that was emerging in the period between 1972 and 1974 was that investment in education needed to be rethought. The high-level manpower crisis that had confronted donors in the previous decade had passed and had been substituted by a crisis of the opposite sort: too many educated people chasing too few appropriate jobs. It was this imbalance between education and employment that had attracted the attention of the great International Labour Office (ILO) Employment Missions to Colombia, Sri Lanka, and Kenya (between 1970 and 1972). The same dilemma was to produce Dore's *Diploma Disease* in 1976. It would lead McNamara in the introduction of the World Bank's *Education: Sector Working Paper* (1974) to say that "it [the policy paper] states convincingly that educational systems in developing countries are all too often ill-conceived and are not adapted to their developmental needs. The educational policies themselves are not always at fault; they have tended to serve only too well the basically irrelevant development strategies they were supposed to uphold and sustain" (World Bank, 1974, p. 1).

THE DISCOVERY OF INFORMATION

This mood of rethinking education within the wider frame of development policies had also lain behind the high-level donor meetings that had taken place in Bellagio in 1972 and 1973, and whose spirit had been captured in the book *Education and Development Reconsidered: The Bellagio Conference Papers* (Ward, 1974). At these meetings attended by the heads of the major agencies, there was a very strong revisionist strain. The age of innocence in which donors merely had expanded the existing ex-colonial provision especially at the higher levels was over. This formula had left the mass of poorer people outside. Out of this disappointment with the past came a feeling that new ways must be found of supporting more appropriate educational development. One of the elements in the new wisdom that emerged was an emphasis on experimentation—the search for new ways of delivering more relevant education and training to more people, preferably at a lower cost. A Bellagio paper argued vigorously that the new donor priorities should be

1. Intensified and expanded applied research, particularly in the developing countries themselves, on alternative educational and informational delivery systems appropriate to the diverse employment needs and opportunities of these nations. . . .

2. Systematic and controlled pilot experimentation with educational innovations emanating from research efforts. Given the risks and costs associated with experimentation, it is unlikely that developing nations will be willing to bear the cost of systematic experimentation. (Edwards and Todaro, 1974, pp. 21–22)

It is well known that one of the consequences of this donor revisionism was a preoccupation with developments outside the realm of the ordinary school—in the world of nonformal education. But less fully documented has been the external support of promising innovations in education in the developing world of the kind that Edwards was pointing to above.

One of the first concrete evidences of this second thread in donor thinking was the collaborative support by seven Bellagio donors to an International Education Reporting Service (IERS). This focused on significant innovations and disseminated information about these through a series of case study booklets that numbered no less than forty in the years between 1975 and 1978. The impression associated with the series was that somehow the information derived from these innovations would have a direct impact on the hard-pressed policy maker and on the policy process. Looking backwards, this may seem rather optimistic:

The principal aim of this service (IERS) is to provide information about innovations which have a high relevance to developing countries. It will be designed to serve educational leaders in such countries, particularly those who decide policies and plan and administer education systems, so that they may be aware of the various possibilities open to them. Thus the IERS is seen as one instrument for helping in the renovation of national systems of education. (Hochleitner, 1978, back cover)

Another approach supported by this same group of donors also involved information, but this time research information. Their decision was that a mechanism should be developed to establish the priority of the flow of resources to critical areas of educational research. The assumption lying behind this idea was that existing research knowledge needed to be reviewed, especially that pertaining to the developing world, and promising avenues identified which could justify further investment. Just as the donors had sought to identify key areas of research in agriculture and in population, so perhaps a similar initiative in education would have a payoff. IDRC, on behalf of the other donors, agreed to fund a Research Review and Advisory Group (RRAG) that would have the following functions:

> The research advisory group would identify research priorities of importance to more than one developing country, commission state-of-the-art reviews, identify areas requiring further research, assist when requested in designing or evaluating research programs, assess national and regional research capacities, and advise on the progress and direction of the research effort as a whole. (IDRC, 1976, p. 13)

This was a pretty tall order. The group was seen as a kind of educational research commission, advising donors and disseminating its findings to the policy community. IDRC funded the initiative in its first phase with over $400,000 Canadian dollars, and the project duly had its first meeting in 177 with twelve group members and two coordination staff members.

Networking and Advice

Although there was a strong priority-setting element within the RRAG agenda, the networking and communication problem was the first to be picked out by Robert Myers, RRAG's first coordinator. He argued that what had been particularly conceived by the donor group to be the problem was poor "communication among disparate parts of the 'educational community' (researchers, practitioners, policy makers, funders)" (Myers, 1981, p. 1). In other words, the donors had already prejudged that one of the priority themes for the group was networking across the different parts of the research and policy community rather than networking among researchers or among policy makers. One part of the design of RRAG, therefore, was intended to deal with this problem. Its composition was made up of five agency people and seven researchers. In this manner it was presumably hoped that the traditional problem of researchers getting their message to policy makers would be alleviated, at least within the group itself.

It is worth emphasizing this aspect of the original RRAG structure, as it is one that continued in the organizational arrangements of several of the successor bodies. Thus, the South East Asia Research Review and Advisory Group (SEAR-

RAG) built into its initial membership just one senior researcher and one senior policy maker per country, and it then added to this formula a third element, a practitioner. And NORRAG described itself in its statutes as "a network of persons committed to improve the quality of interactions among research, policy and practice in the North, as a means to support education and training in the South" (NORRAG, 1992, Article 2).

In both cases, as in the original RRAG, the notion is that, where there is a problem of communication, the parties are included as the core membership of the organization. This formula was not quite the same in the case of the Educational Research Network in Eastern and Southern Africa (ERNESA), which decided that its core membership would consist of nationwide organizations of educational research cum documentation. ERNESA also decided, however, that there could be five individual members, of which one must be a policy maker, one a practitioner, one a documentalist and one a researcher. So, again, some emphasis on bringing into the same RRAG group members of the different communities.

The composition of the original RRAG group implied two kinds of networking. First, the group itself was a network with a particular chemistry, including the need for researchers and policy people to work together on the same very demanding agenda. It was very important also that membership should be from both the North and the South (seven of the original twelve members were from the South). Hence, the networking within the group should be North-South as well as South-South.

Second, the results of the group's activities were meant to be networked to the donor community and to researchers and policy makers. As a group, with quite considerable resources for meeting and exchanging materials, it might be possible for RRAG to overcome, for itself, the traditional barriers between research and policy, and between Northern and Southern research. But would it really be able to do anything about the fundamental problem that had lain behind its formation: that a great deal of research had been done over the years in the developing world, but that very little was known about its quality, its implications for investment, or the gaps that might still be there? The real attraction the RRAG concept had for many of the donors, including its sponsor, IDRC, was that it promised to sort out what the state of the art was in existing and required research, and to synthesize what had been done and prioritize what still needed to be done.

The State-of-the-Art Review as an Archetypal RRAG Mechanism

The double R at the beginning of the acronym, RRAG, underlines this key feature of its intended activity. It was not meant to *do* research but to review research and then to advise on what the consequences were for donors and national governments. Originally, this research review was meant to be done in six main areas that had already been identified in a series of meetings in 1974 and 1975. They are worth mentioning in order to understand the scale of what was expected of the RRAG process: (1) learning efficiency, (2) education and employment, (3) imbalances in educational opportunities, (4) planning, management, and administration, (5) cost and finance, (6) evaluation (IDRC, 1976, p. 7).

The assumptions about knowledge that initially lay behind RRAG were very much influenced by the model of agriculture (or population) science. The model assumed that an eminent group could objectively review, synthesize, and then generalize about the state of information on any one of these six areas. This could be done with sufficient authority to guide investment. The state-of-the-art review would be the crucial vehicle for RRAG to adopt. The attraction of this model was that it appeared to offer a way of sorting out and synthesizing scientifically what research had been done, and, more rapidly than in a regular research project, coming up with conclusions for policy. Whether all the RRAG members were aware of this or not, it was the very mechanism that the World Bank's education policy group had also just identified as useful for steering their own investments in education.

The World Bank and IDRC/RRAG are mentioned together because they came up with fundamentally different approaches and conclusions to the task of carrying out a research review. For example, both the Bank and RRAG reviewed the area of teacher effectiveness in the mid-to-late 1970s, but their methods and conclusions were different. A research review is not at all like a scientific measuring instrument and is intimately affected by the value assumptions and attitudes about knowledge of the individuals and institutions who carry out the review.

The conclusion of the RRAG-sponsored review of teacher effectiveness (which had looked at hundreds of studies in very different cultural contexts) adopted the following tone:

> Are the results of this review disappointing? From the perspective of secure guidelines for policy, they may be. The review has not come up with startling facts, nor did it confirm or refute in a definite way commonly held assumptions; it has not been able to assert that "this is what will work in these circumstances." But from the perspective of finding out what goes on in teacher research in the Third World and even more than that, of finding out whether there are indications of some agreements and a road to follow, it is a positive review. (Avalos and Haddad, 1981, p. 60)

The World Bank study on teacher training and student achievement in less developed countries examined just thirty-two research reports which were "legitimate and valid empirical studies of student achievement which met the necessary criteria" (Husén, Saha, and Noonan, 1978, p. 9). It was then possible to make a number of generalizations about teacher qualifications and teacher attitudes. Even so, the consultants on the Bank study had been aware of the importance of culture and context, and this 1978 set of conclusions was still much less confident than the recommendations that would be associated with later Bank reports. For instance, in the Bank paper, *Education in Sub-Saharan Africa*, ten years later, the section on teacher training produced much more prescriptive recommendations: "The following kinds of investment are not likely to have any noticeable effect on primary school quality despite their potentially high cost: reducing class size, providing primary teachers with more than a general secondary education, providing teachers with more than minimal exposure to pedagogical theory" (World Bank, 1988, p. 60).

The much greater diffidence in the RRAG review of teacher effectiveness pointed to something much more contradictory in the approach of RRAG to its original mandate of synthesizing and sorting out research in the developing world to allow for more rational investment. The members of the group did not consider it appropriate to try to decide at a world level on what works and what doesn't work in educational research, experimentation, and innovation. They were not attracted by the temptation of making transnational generalizations, but instead turned to examine the specificity of the research environments and research cultures in the developing world (see, for example, Shaeffer and Nkinyangi, 1983).

The reason for going into this early discussion of a project that was virtually seen by its sponsors as an education research commission for the developing world is that the RRAG members' retreat from this particular interpretation of an international advisory group had importance for later developments. In particular, the emphasis by members of the group on the specificity of research cultures at the regional level (which had been reinforced by the case studies done for the research environments study in 1981) was the starting point for what would shortly become the regionalization of RRAG.

The reasons for moving, between 1981 and 1985, from an international network of twelve people to a regional approach are several, but among the most influential were those that related to representativeness, dissemination, and networking. In the original RRAG, for example, there had been just one member from Africa, Tunde Yoloye from Nigeria, and just one member from Latin America, Ernesto Schiefelbein from Chile. Similarly, there had been just one member from the Caribbean, one from South Asia, and none from the Middle East. This structure of just one person for a whole continent might have been acceptable if the task was seen as a commission functioning for a short time to turn the spotlight on research needs and priorities worldwide. But if the mandate was also advice and networking, not just to IDRC or to the donors, but to national research bodies and national governments in the developing world, then the idea of twelve wise men and women operating as an ongoing mechanism at the international level would be difficult to reconcile with national or regional impact.

This was the thinking that produced the first regional RRAG in South East Asia (SEARRAG) in 1982 and the Educational Research Network in Eastern and Southern Africa (ERNESA) in 1985. It also led to the idea of a Northern Research Review and Advisory Group (NORRAG) in 1985. In Latin America, Red de Investigacion, an informal network to exchange abstracts, had been set up as early as 1972. As it grew, it also began to stress the link between educational research and decision making and was renamed REDUC (Cariola et al. 1987).

THE NORRAG CULTURE OF NETWORKING:
ESSENTIAL HISTORY

The first NORRAG meeting drew upon those who had been involved in the staff work and membership of the original RRAG group. This meant that at the launch meeting for NORRAG in Stockholm in 1985, there were the following:

Kenneth King (Edinburgh, United Kingdom), Beatrice Avalos (Cardiff, United Kingdom), and Noel McGinn (Harvard, United States). There were also present members of the International Institute of Education of the University of Stockholm. And closely linked to the Institute were a number of people associated with the Swedish International Development Agency (SIDA). As the network developed in the months after the launch, the notion grew that there was a particular role for a RRAG group based in the North to deal with donor-agency information and to make this available to other RRAG groups in the South. Initially it was this brokerage role of the network that commended NORRAG to SIDA for funding. The character of the early NORRAG network is well captured in the very first issue of *NORRAG News*:

> Access to information about the donor agencies and about major research initiatives developed in the North had always been a part of the RRAG agenda and so with regionalization it became natural to explore whether there was some way in which the extraordinary range of donor activities (meetings, innovations, policy papers, etc.) could be made more available to RRAG groups in the South and to other donors. The mechanism that has been developed to try to do this is a Northern RRAG group, consisting of two or three members in each of the main donor countries. This network has just begun to be formed in 1986, and can be seen as an informal support group for transferring to colleagues in South RRAG groups the very latest information on meetings, strategy papers and new research priorities. To do this effectively, Northern RRAG members need to have good working relations with the bilateral agencies and multilateral agencies located in their countries, as well as good links with academic and professional associations. The primary concern of the Northern RRAG group is with the improvement of North-South communication. (NORRAG News, 1986, p. 4)

It can be seen from this brief description that the original NORRAG saw itself, as did its principal funder, as having a service role in respect of the Southern RRAGs. In part this derived from a desire by the original NORRAG members to be responsive to what their colleagues in Southern networks suggested at the launch meeting of NORRAG. But over time, and in discussion with the other networks, it was decided that NORRAG should seek to operate in the same way as other RRAG groups; in other words, it should develop and pursue those priorities it feels to be important. If these are well done, they will almost by definition be of value to the other networks, without having to justify them as being "for the benefit of the South" (King, 1991a, p. 6).

In July 1992, NORRAG shifted from being an informal group to one that had a constitution, and membership was opened to all individuals and organizations who were interested in NORRAG objectives. Apart from its own membership, it still directed its news bulletin to all the main contact points of the Southern RRAG networks in South East Asia, East and Southern Africa, and Latin America, as well as to other research centers.

Reviewing Future Options for NORRAG

NORRAG draws its current membership principally from researchers and agencies, in other words, from different cultures of research and of policy. NORRAG is a secondary organization consisting of individuals drawn from different kinds of primary organizations which have the principal claims on members' time.

As to the kind of discourse that NORRAG (and *NORRAG News*) encourages among this diverse membership, it is not so much one which speaks of researchers influencing decision makers or policy makers in the way that was commonplace when the original RRAG was founded. It is closer to a conversation in which both agency and research people analyze a common problem. Thus, if you examine the last six or seven numbers of *NORRAG News*, you will see that there are a variety of agency and research viewpoints pulled together within a particular number.

Sharing a common platform from time to time does not make for a common culture, however. Nor does the fact that agency and research people jointly helped to define NORRAG's constitution necessarily give both groups a sense of ownership of the organization. To develop the intimate conversation necessary to achieve shared understandings of the problems we are trying to address requires value judgments. It is not a mechanism for offering some objective facts about educational development. Consider the first paragraph of the statutes of NORRAG: "NORRAG is a network of persons *committed* [emphasis added] to improve the quality of interactions amongst research, policy and practice in the North as a means to support education and training in the South" (NORRAG, 1992).

This first statement about commitment is followed up in Article 6 by more detailed objectives and strategies using terms that emphasize that NORRAG intends to take a value position on education, training, and development: "critical analysis . . . collaborative research . . . advocacy of education and training policies . . . co-operation with other RRAG networks . . . share information . . . join efforts in advocacy" (NORRAG, 1992).

This discourse of commitment, collaboration, critical analysis, and advocacy needs to be grounded in a view about the development of education and training in the North and South, and more generally in a view about development itself. This is not to say that all NORRAG members need to subscribe to a particular version of development or development theory. But it may nevertheless be important to lay out in a future issue or issues of *NORRAG News* what are the perspectives on development that underpin this commitment, information dissemination, advocacy, and advice.

It is clear that the original RRAG was expected to take on a much more ambitious program of functions than a group of twelve part-time people could possibly achieve. The regional RRAGs have started with more modest goals. They have all, however, retained a view from the original RRAG that they should not so much do research as review, synthesize, and comment on research. Also they all would appear in some fashion to have retained the view that the worlds of policy, research, and practice need to be brought closer together. Perhaps as important as anything, each network appears to have retained a commitment to the importance of the role of the individual person—whether in Tanzania or Uganda, Holland or Sweden, Chile or Mexico, Malaysia or Thailand. REDUC has had a twenty-year association with particular individuals in the coordinating center in Chile, and there are other examples from the other networks of relatively long-term personal commitments to the ideal.

So it is that ideal that should be revisited, for networking is not an end in itself. As it frames its program of activities for the coming year, NORRAG needs to look very seriously at some of the basic questions about networking and development discussed elsewhere in this book. But in doing so, it may need to look beyond itself at comparable experience elsewhere.

For example, now that the four regional RRAG networks have each been established for quite some time, and each has developed its own agenda, it may be worth asking whether they see themselves as having any element of common purpose. In a world that is still struggling unsuccessfully with general agreements on trade between North and North, and North and South, is there any suggestion that such regional organizations should develop a wider agenda? What, for instance, would a general agreement on networking for educational development look like?

FROM GROUP TO NETWORK: MANAGEMENT ISSUES

Michel Carton

NORRAG's transformation, in 1992, into a network of the associative type provides an excellent opportunity to define with more precision the notion of network. The concept is fashionable today but, like all trends, in fields as varied as interpersonal psychology, sociology, geography, history, engineering, urban management, mathematics, and even more, network is in fact an old notion.

In French the equivalent of network, *réseau*, originates from the Latin *retis*, "net." The *réseuil* (nowadays: *résille*, "hairnet") referred, as from the Renaissance, to a net women used to keep their hair up. During the seventeenth century the word *réseau* was a technical and popular term used by weavers and wickerworkers to qualify the warp and woof of textile or vegetable fibers. The notion developed during the eighteenth century in a military context for engineering and fortifications. It is during the nineteenth century that doctors started talking about the *réseau sanguin*, "blood stream," and that topographers used the notion of network referring to space triangulation.[1] Today, network has become a concept used not only in technical fields (territory, communications), but also organizational fields (network firms) and social fields (relation networks, information circuits). This discussion pays attention only to the social dimension of networks—"networks are nothing if they are not social networks" (Mulgan, 1991, p. 6)—without neglecting of course that relations cannot be established without technical supports.

Analyzing society in terms of networks is a recent trend, about forty years old if we do not include J. L. Moreno's sociometric approach in 1934. Barnes (1969) followed by Bott (1971) are the first to have proposed to overrule the structuralist-functionalist tendency. "Rather than starting off with a classification—a priori—of the observable world into a series of discontinued classifications, they start off with a set of relations from which they branch off figurations and social structure typologies. They therefore put forward propositions starting off from the whole to the parts of structures, from relations to categories and, in fine, from behaviors to attitudes." (Ferrand, 1987, p. 37)

In contrast with sociologists who stick to describing the structures of relations linking members of social systems, network specialists choose a behaviorist and inductive approach to analyze concrete social relations without taking into consideration norms and cultural particulars. This links them with the defenders of the sociology of actors (e.g., Crozier, Friedburg, Sansaulieu, Touraine) and of practices (e.g., de Certeau, Goffman). With this outlook it seems possible to overcome the limits, related to structuralism, given by concepts referring to fixed references such as center, culture, and function. Structures exist but are not congealed; organizations are in perpetual motion as revealed by the analysis of concrete social relations between specific actors.

> Social systems can be apprehended from the viewpoint of networks, and furthermore can be considered as being nothing else than networks of networks. This approach enables us to understand better how internal and external relations are articulated and mutually altered. Network analyzing therefore becomes an essential key for sociologists who admit that social structures can be represented as networks, a set of "nodes" (elements of the social system) and as a set of lines figuring the connections between the elements. This observation of social interrelations enables us to object to the idea that social systems are only a collection of individuals, or of dyads and restricted groups, or furthermore of simple categories. It is, in other words, the opposite of descriptive sociology: the subject of the discipline is situated at the level of concrete modes of social functioning within a given scale. The *nodes* [emphasis added] can represent individuals but also groups, households, communities, firms, States. . . . The links can represent flows of various nature: information, resources, relations (respect, friendship, influence, power, domination . . .). (Bakis, 1993, p. 102)

TECHNICAL NETWORKS

Nodes, flow lines: it is necessary now to rapidly define these terms featuring the network approach, particularly in the technical field. A network is first of all a thread arranging points (or summits) and lines (or curves, connections, tracks). The question is whether these significant points are linked to others according to a specific design, a certain typology. If this approach is applied to geography, different types of networks are possible: branch networks, circuit networks, and barrier networks. On a map a network materializes as infrastructures, itineraries, and surfaces (stitches or cells).

If, up to now, the visible topological aspects of networks have often been privileged by a geography of distances, a geography of temporal accessibility is now fundamental for the analysis and practice of networks: the circulation periods of flows, of products and information, within networks reveal but also act as agents of spatial differentiation by creating disparities (inequalities in access to the network) or by reinforcing these inequalities with an always better service regarding the most favored parts of the space considered.

NORRAG could fall into the same trap. It could become one more network that increases disparate access to information by and on the South; and it could also make it more difficult for people in the South to produce their own information. NORRAG's wish is to be both a social network that organizes meetings between members, and an information network. At the same time, it seeks to balance geography of distances and geography of temporal accessibility.

The rest of my comments are addressed to this issue. System and network can be viewed as two antinomic concepts. "Networks, as opposed to systems, are not hierarchical. A network does not regulate its boundaries with the environment, but instead participates in the regulation of the system's boundaries" (Dupuy, 1985, p. 84).

On the one hand, structures of the NORRAG type (e.g., South East Asia Research Review and Advisory Group, Educational Research Network in Eastern and Southern Africa, Red Latinoamericana de Informacion y Documentación en Education) are each minisystems, in as much as they have their own features: autonomy, stability, coherence, and organization. On the other hand, their purposes are clearly to put in touch with each other individual or collective actors who are related to the bigger systems—universities, assistance agencies, and NGOs—each of which has its own network. Systems and networks are therefore different concepts but dialectically linked in so far as the dynamism of the system largely depends on identifiable variables (among others) in the whole network: connectability, connectivity, homogeneity, and nodality.

Connectability is a topological concept used to characterize the network of relations between subsystems of a territorial system. NORRAG will have strong connectability if it manages to put into direct and close touch a great many individuals in universities, agencies, and NGOs (see Figure 1).

Connectivity characterizes the multiplicity of the bonds established in the system throughout the network, direct relations as well as alternative relations. NORRAG will have a high rating in connectivity if it enables one of its members in an

Figure 1
Connectability

A Network with No Connectability

A Network with High Connectability

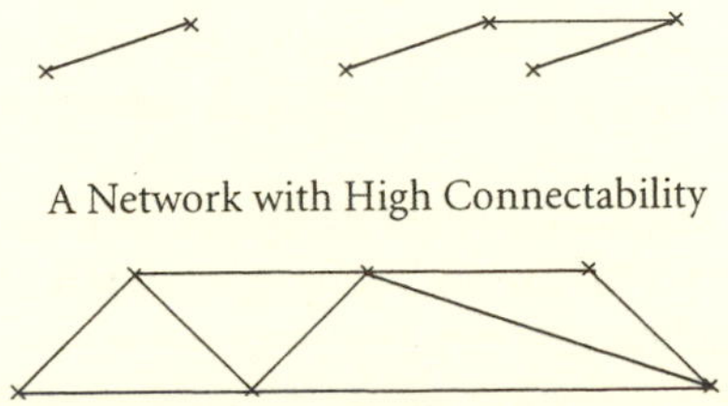

Figure 2
Connectivity

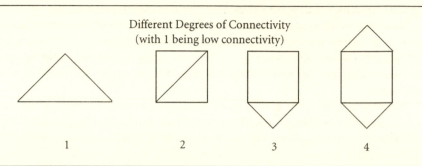

Different Degrees of Connectivity
(with 1 being low connectivity)

1   2   3   4

---

organization to get in contact with another member by contacts with other members who also will gain from the connection (see Figure 2).

Homogeneity refers to "the fact that the way different elements of the system depend on each other through the intermediary of the network is independent of the particular features of the bonds considered" (Dupuy, 1985, p. 85). Therefore, NORRAG will have achieved a high degree of homogeneity when the working relationships established between members are common across members. A newsletter is characteristic of this.

Finally, *nodality* reflects the way each node or member of the network can establish relations with others. The degree of nodality reflects the intensity of the contributions of a network's members. In the example of a newsletter, articles submitted by members provide the means to form linkages with other members.

FIRM NETWORKING AND SOCIAL-POLITICAL NETWORKING

It may seem that these four variables can be applied only to a fixed number of members of the network. If so, this would contradict NORRAG's aim to influence a maximum, but unspecified, number of actors working in the field of education and training for the South. One way to resolve this apparent problem is to think of "opening" a network.

If the notion of system assumes hierarchy and the notion of structure a center of functioning, in which center implies enclosure and finality, then networks could be conceived with or without centers, open or closed. The uncentered approach belongs to the philosopher, Serres: "By definition, within a network no point is privileged compared to any other, no point is univocally subordinated to such or such" (Serres, 1968, p. 11). This open approach also belongs to the philosopher Derrida. He notes that even an apparently rigid structure such as a beam is in fact "an assembling that has the structure of a braid, a weaving, a crossing that will let go of different threads and different lines of force, or of meaning, as much as it will be able to knot others" (Derrida, 1972, p. 4).

From this point of view one must simultaneously conceive and operate, inside and outside of the network: a network can incorporate other points at each of its endings in such a way that any description of the status of the set of points appears as a principle of complex and off-centered organization, achieved for the sake of the analysis and the action, but for which we simultaneously think of external connections.

The debate on the center of the network then becomes crucial: how can we assure at the same time important degrees of connectability, connectivity, homogeneity, and nodality between the members of a network while continually retaining open the wish and the possibility to extend or link up the network? Can this be assured spontaneously?

The world of enterprise and its recent development gives elementary answers, as it is especially tempting to consider universities, agencies, and NGOs as development firms all working in the same market of international assistance to education and training!

Networking and Firms

In the world of enterprise, the concept of network is principally used to point out a new trend of relations between firms. In the classical outlook it was considered that the organization of productive socialization operated in two ways: through the market or through vertical integration (merging, concentration), that is, "Buy or make." Both these processes, however, have now reached their limits as much for technical reasons as for commercial or organizational reasons. The network, situated between market and dependency (related to the integration), then appears as an intermediary between firms that are juridically and financially independent, but linked up (not only commercially) in a relationship of cooperation, collaboration, and partnership.

The "firms" of NORRAG could fit into this diagram: agencies, universities, and NGOs are independent entities but "partners." Does this mean, however, that there is no relationship of dependency between them, as opposed to what Serres requires?

The ambiguity of the concept of network appears, for instance, in the case of subcontracting networks between firms such as NGOs and universities. It often is the case that one firm subcontracts with another only after the funding agency fails in its effort to integrate them by developing its own research centers and secular arms in the form of NGOs. Does networking, as in NORRAG, reflect a more spontaneous participation process, or rather a provoked participation, using Meister's (1978) terms? For example, it is obvious that NORRAG is the product of the initiative of individuals who share common visions and objectives regarding international education and who want to participate in bringing it into operation, but NORRAG also is the product of the support of certain cooperative agencies, such as the Swedish International Development Agency (SIDA) and the International Development Research Centre (IDRC). They participate critically in their thoughtful contributions to NORRAG but also control the financial terms of their own and others' participation.[2]

Up to now the members of NORRAG have been considered as individuals belonging to autonomous firms; the latter could also be considered as departments of the same big firm producing international education. If a firm is defined as a complex set of heterogenous elements, how can these elements communicate horizontally and directly to the outside? Different practices and cultures get in the way. But this communication is important, as it supplies the social corpus, that is, the firm with information (and decisions) that affect its ability to function. Today this information must be supplied in short lapses of time in order to take into consideration the complexity, the differentiation, and the changeability of the markets in which the firm operates. How then should this communication be started: should it be organized by a hierarchical center, such as the World Bank, or can it emerge out of networking?

> Networking consists in putting in intensive touch components often hetero-genous and of different logic and practices (even if they belong to the same firm). Most often the components preexist the networking, because this networking does not have the almost compulsory feature of cooperation versus division of labor. In other words networking can be considered as a *voluntary* act of the components whose motive would be the *advantage* (economic, but also more generally symbolic, affective, etc.) that they draw from it. Because of this the network should be considered as *labile*, in other words evanescent and likely to be self-destructive as soon as the advantage (or the perception of such an advantage) disappears. This is the paradoxical feature of network which, while remaining labile, insists in existing at long-range in order that the advantage that justifies the investment (economic, moral or affective) may bear its fruit. Indeed the result of networking is scarcely immediate because between the project, the motive or the desire for the network and the positive effect of the network there is a long period of *latency* during which the actors grope about, try to understand each other, adjust their expressions and practices. It's the famous training in transac-tional analysis. There are similarities with Habermas's analysis on intersub-jective understanding that requires a common cultural and linguistic basis in order to establish communication. During this training phase it is not all the components or individuals of a component that take part in a network, but most often only a share that comprises the interface: we recognize here M. Callons' (1989) spokesmen or *innovating nodes* that we have disclosed in small and medium institutions with paradoxical innovation. Analyzing the inter-faces is essential for analyzing networks as their quality and mobility depend on the efficiency of the network. (Durand, 1992, pp. 1–5)

This approach refers to the features of the network as identified by Landier (1991):

1. A network is always based on a strong interpersonal relationship that is well beyond the work itself. It isn't just anybody in a firm (or from one firm to another) that speaks to anyone. . . . Moreover, in networking logic, the global efficiency results from the quality and the fullness of interper-sonal relationship rather than from the skills characteristic of each of its members considered individually.

2. Interpersonal relationships in a network have informal features. They don't result from implementing procedures, applying guidelines or executing instructions, but from a cooperation freely agreed upon based on trust. . . .

3. These relations are not hierarchical. The network puts in touch autonomous individuals, and beyond them entities, independent from each other. In a network there is not therefore a unique center for decisions but as many centers of decisions as entities taking part. In the case of one of these entities trying to dominate the others and claiming to enforce its own rules or its own purposes, the network ceases to be a network and tends to structure as a traditional pyramidal organization. . . .

4. A network comprises a progressive and open feature, departures being rarely formally and definitely observed, except in the case of breaking up induced by a breach of rules. On the other hand the rules progress bearing in mind the accumulation of shared experiences within the network. Finally the nature and the intensity of the relationship between different members of the network progresses according to circumstances.

5. The absence of hierarchy within the network does not mean a chaotic situation in so far that step by step a process of self-regulation occurs. (Landier, 1991, p. 120)

Networking and African States

It is interesting to bring together these features of networks in postmodern societies in the way Deleuze and Guattari (1976) and Bayart (1989) analyze the functioning of African states. These are seen not as autonomous entities of the civil society but as intrinsically related to it through the intermediation of social-political factions implementing ethnic, religious, parental, economic valences in ad hoc networks entrusted to solve specific problems. In this view conflicts between factions are not a sign of the disintegration of society but, on the contrary, a mode of production of political life in that these factions control both the state and the networks they shape.

Finally, the postcolonial state lives more like a rhizome than like a radicular set:

In order to be endowed with its own historicity it does not unfurl on one dimension, from a genetic trunk, like a majestic oak tree that thrusts its roots deep into the fundamental humus of History. It is an ever-changing multiplicity of networks whose underground stems link up scattered points of the society. Understanding it requires that we go beyond examining its aerial parts, the institutional buds, in order to examine its adventitious roots, to analyze the bulbs and tubers from which it secretly feeds from and pulls out its strength. Let us also be "weary of the tree," of this arborescent conception of the State: in truth it has exhausted theoreticians. . . . It is better to devote to the study of the intelligence "of stems and filaments" that look like roots, or better still that connect up with them by penetrating in the trunk, free to make use of them as new strange purposes. (Deleuze & Guattari, 1974, pp. 45–46)

The factional organization of African societies is also noted by Bayart:

All these mechanisms refer more or less to the realm of networking. They echo back a global organization of African societies that a great many studies on trade, savings, wages, migration, parenthood testify about. And, as such, they imply that so unfolds the talent of political entrepreneur knowing how to fasten up without release the skein of ceaseless bargaining, capable of rationally managing their material and symbolic resources to the best of their own benefit and that of the community that gives them fame and influence, suited to mobilizing the forces of the Word, of passion and anxiety, should it be in the nocturnal world of the invisible, and finally scholars in the same white knowledge the contemporary State claims to be from. . . . For lack of a true structuring in social classes, the predominance of big men at the head of networks continues indeed to be circumstantial and, for a decisive part, to be dependent on the fulfillment of individual performances. (Bayart, 1989, pp. 272–273, 268)

Aren't the "big" men of African networks actually filling the function of coordination regulation that Durand analyzed in firms?

Self-regulation between units does not seem be able to be carried out "naturally," in other words through the only *autopoïese* of F. Varela. The natural balance in a social (or entirely automatic) setting seems impossible to reach without the existence of a coordination function. Hence the necessity to devise a *coordination unit* perfectly informed thanks to the work of the information dispatcher and taking the steady decisions that are imperative.

Dynamic programmable coordination refers to the flexible ordering impulse that guarantees the coherence of the interventions of different units. Each term has its significance. "Dynamic" means that the priority system that affects the coherence of the interventions must always be in a situation of watchfulness, in other words likely to be reconfigured in order to ensure at the most the appropriateness between situation and structure in order to obtain organizational efficiency.

"Programmable" refers to the technical device able to collect, to transmit and to process information originating from the environment. It is not only a question of the local networks, functional components of communication, but also artificial intelligence systems conceived in order to record the constant change of the environment and to analyze it, while reasoning in order to detect the combination or the decision circuit best suited at such or such a moment. The main problem is not to transform both these functions and

units, *information dispatchers and coordinators*, into new hierarchial functions. (Durand, 1992, pp. 13–14, emphasis in original)

NETWORKING IN THE NORTH, STRUCTURES IN THE SOUTH?

I do not propose that NORRAG with its 150 members spread across agencies,
universities, and NGOs could be compared with this coordination unit between the
units of the "International Education" firm or with the African faction networks.
However, is it possible to prevent members from perceiving the coordination and
the production of *NORRAG News* as the purpose of a center and not as the fruit of
the network's functioning, making the network a mere structure? The nature and
the functions of the executive committee, the coordination, and the newsletter
deserve to be analyzed in the light of the previous considerations. On the other
hand, the importance of interpersonal and informal relations in the birth and the
functioning of a firm network (see Landier, above) is to be found in the history of
NORRAG (by going back to the original Research Review and Advisory Group in
1977) and justifies the choice made in 1992, when the coordination function was
formalized, to keep up individual membership within the network.

This choice also reveals ambiguity in the concept of network and the difficulty
in associating the latter with the necessity of coordination. Indeed, how, within a
network, can what comprises the essential value of the relations in the group—their
informality—be protected? Without going into the details of a debate on informality, it can be emphasized that, in the field of present interest, the qualifier "informal"
ends up specifying at the same time the nature of the information exchanged, the
communication situations, and the relations between speakers. As a matter of fact,
nowadays, informality, both in firms as in assistance work, is essential for the success
of a product or a project in that

> Knowledge, learning, scientific and technical know-how comprise the imma-
> terial components, more and more important, in producing a satellite just as
> in reforming an educational system;

> Increasing requirements of integration, of overlapping of science, technology
> and production appear and it is henceforth impossible to analyze their
> relations with sequential and linear lapses of time, what educational planning
> did, for instance, during the 1950s;

> The social actors, taken individually, therefore become decisive as they are in
> possession of knowledge that is not totally reducible to achieved knowledge,
> knowledge that becomes indissociable from them and that can only be
> valorized through their spatial physical and/or social nearness. (May, 1992)

If some authors then use spatial nearness as a sine qua non condition of
networking, others insist more on the importance of the trust and complicity of
informal relations between members just as much as their realizations in a feebly

institutionalized cooperation relationship. It is then obvious that the existence of memberships and/or of common references is essential for the development of networks. Does NORRAG have sufficient common basis, drawn up during the years within a group, to be a true network? It is important not to fall into the trap of the diminished view that a network only performs on the basis of cooperation and partnership; a network, inside and outside, is squashed between rivalry and competitiveness. The blooming of North-South networks and South-South networks is an illustration of this.

This competitiveness between networks raises the issue now in debate about the globalization of RRAG networks. In regard to economics, globalization is in its third phase: it started off with the internationalization of export streams; it continued with the transnationalization of investment streams; and it proceeds now with worldwide production and information networking. These are not based any longer on global firms, in other words totally integrated structures, but on cooperative relationships between multinational network firms. Moreover, the end of the Cold War reveals new regional centers (South East Asia and China, North America, and Western and Eastern Europe).

Isn't the original RRAG, created in 1977, from which these firms operate, an international firm? Are the different RRAGs (NORRAG, SEARRAG, ERNESA, REDUC), born from it, transnational regional organizations displaying spatial and political division of the North-South dependency system of the 1970s? Should they now associate within an international network firm with partners contractually linked for a certain amount of common aims but competing with others? A critical topic of discussion is whether NORRAG belongs to the North, as implied by its name. How far are the RRAGs from functioning like the scientific, technical, or political networks of the North that permit organizations producing goods or powers to adapt quickly to changes in their environment?

Turning back to Africa (which could in fact be considered progressive with its many networks), it is a question of understanding what the concept of modern network means, as it is carried out by ERNESA and since 1993, by Educational Research Network for Western and Central Africa (ERNWACA; ROCARE, Réseau Ouest et Central Africain de Recherche en Éducation). Can these networks be something other than the instruments of the various factions mentioned above? What can they do faced with a situation where "being used as a means of protecting acquired benefits and of gaining dominant positions, used as a political and trade-union springboard or, more commonly, favoring to obtain more or less respectable personal advantages, the field of education rarely has the internal institutional capability up to the standards of the ambitions of its development objectives, at least those that are officially declared by those who decide" (Hallak & Tobelem, 1993, p. 2).

Should they aim, as opposed to the networks of the North based on antitaylorism, for a better division of labor in the field of education and training by creating professional cadre as well as researchers? Can they aim at developing structures, when this last term is often associated with the state and presented by assistance agencies that finance the network, and is often identified as *the* cause of the crisis? Can they remain informal and self-organized according to the international trend, or should they dodge these notions that the North handles without really knowing what they mean in Africa?

Only the future will be able to tell if the North should be unstructured into networks or if the South's networks should become structured.

NOTES

1. Names such as Vauban (1678), the abbot La Caille (1751), and L. Lalanne (1863) should be remembered as forerunners in this field.

2. This calls to mind the issue raised by Gramsci regarding the autonomy of organic intellectuals and their functions in political and social life.

AFRICA

PART IV

Efforts to develop networks that link researchers and policy makers seem to have been less successful in Africa than in other regions. The first two chapters in this section explore reasons why this might be so. A third chapter counters their assertions. These three chapters are a rich source of elements for explaining the contexts that determine the survival and effectiveness of networks that deal in information.

Hoppers suggests that the model of networking transferred from the Northern RRAG experience is inappropriate for the African context.[1] First, as Namuddu also comments, African researchers in general lack the basic infrastructure required for the level of frequency of communication that sustains a network. It is hard enough to get research done, let alone to find the means to share it with other researchers and policy makers.

But, Hopper notes, this is more a problem at the individual level than at the institutional level. Some institutions have been successful in developing and maintaining networks. The Northern RRAG model brings together autonomous individuals, not institutional representatives. In Africa political and economic constraints make this a less effective option than linking institutions together. The institutions in question are primarily state-funded universities. Hoppers questions whether the assumption that the development of network implies and is favored by a withering of the state is necessarily true, or only a feature of a particular historical situation. In Africa it might be that development of communication networks will proceed best by working with state institutions, rather than associations of private individuals.

Namuddu elaborates on reasons why the Northern RRAG model has not lived up to expectations in Africa. In addition to economic and technological constraints, communication in many countries in Africa has suffered from political structures that discourage the free flow of information. Even more difficult are traditions that structure communication by the age and social status of individuals. Namuddu observes that exaggerated standards of methodological rigor limit who can be trusted as a communicant. All these factors have impact when networks are organized as associations of individuals.

Both Namuddu and Hoppers suggest that donor interventions have contributed to the failure of information networks. Namuddu points out that the absence of indigenous communication networks should be taken as evidence of fundamental constraints that must be addressed first. Hoppers claims that donors have favored individuals over institutions.

But not all experiences have been negative. A regional network of national networks (ERNESA—the Educational Research Network in Eastern and Southern Africa) has been in existence for nine years, encouraging research, communication between researchers and policy makers, and formation of linkages with networks outside the region. The twelve countries in the region are highly disparate in terms of colonial experience, current political structure, economic performance, and cultural traditions. Almost all operate with severely constrained resources. Nyati-Ramahobo's detailed description of ERNESA suggests that the network survives because of the highly felt need for communication, deeply rooted in cultural traditions of mutual aid which, incidentally, are not too different than those described by Dubbledam for other regions of the world. Perhaps the telling factor in the ERNESA case is the high commitment to education in all the countries of the region. In some cases this commitment is at the institutional level, in other cases at the individual level. Both contribute to networking.

The next set of chapters in this section describes what various networks have done, and their relative successes and failures. Nyati-Ramahobo's enthusiasm is tempered by a more critical analysis by Komba. His description of ERNESA raises the issue of where the formalization of networks should begin. Should each country first develop a strong national network linking researchers and policy makers? Is a regional network nothing more than a collection of representatives from the national networks? What is the balance between institutionalization and stimulation of contacts among individuals?

The African Educational Research Network (AERN) described briefly by Ploghoft is an example of a network linking institutions. Ploghoft notes the difficulties in the generation of a collegial pattern of communication in a move toward a more horizontal organization. Not only does this run up against bureaucratic traditions within the universities, but a confederacy form of organization multiplies the problem of funding. AERN has continued to thrive because of the commitment of individuals more than institutions. Initially highly placed university officials were critical; now it is the action of graduate student members that gives the organization vitality. The creation of an electronic information exchange has eased some problems and AERN has developed a number of activities linking institutions and individual students and professors.

Sifuna describes the high level of activity of the Educational Research Network in Kenya (ERNIKE), which is associated with ERNESA. Dependence on a single funder is noted with some trepidation. Another national organization, the Botswana Educational Research Association (BERA), has now progressed to the point at which it finances some of its activities through consultancy services provided to the National Commission of Education.

In South Africa the most important networks in education were organized in opposition to the apartheid government's policies. Some of these, like EduSource in Johannesburg, are funded by independent foundations like the Education Foundation. University-based networks emerged only with the first steps to move toward a democratic society in 1990. Gilmour's and Badcock-Walters's chapters were written before the elections: we can imagine that there will be many changes in the near future.

The section ends with a chapter by Michel Carton that returns to the conceptual issues raised at the beginning. Carton tests the hypotheses of Hoppers and Na-muddu in the experience of French-speaking West Africa. Can networks develop when the state is weak? Are institutions alternative homes for networks? Carton argues that the African state is more like a rhizome, with multiple centers each capable of growth, than like a root system with a strong central core. The organization of the state as a collection of factions makes it difficult to keep associations of professionals, and the networks they may develop, out of the political process. If true, then networks in Africa can be expected to have more impact on policy than in other societies in which there is a clearer distinction between the state and civil society.

NOTE

1. This same assertion is made for Asia by Cheng Kai-ming in this volume.

NETWORKING WHEN
THE STATE AND HIGHER
EDUCATION SYSTEMS ARE WEAK

Wim Hoppers

When in the mid-1980s the idea of networking gained popularity in international educational research, there were only vague notions as to what this was all about. As educational researchers in the North we thought about initiatives that would transcend the artificial boundaries of institutions. These initiatives would inspire like-minded colleagues to share intellectual property and use it to generate countervailing power to upstage prevailing academic and policy traditions. We also thought that networking could help researchers to penetrate into the foreign lands of ministries of education, policy committees, training boards, and program or institutional management. With the birth of the RRAG groups and related networks, somehow this vague ideology got mixed up with the practicalities of doing research and of doing something with research in parts of the developing world. The more mundane concerns in East Africa, for example, were how to get into viable research work in the first place, how to get access to the very scarce commodity of information from or about research, and how to penetrate the promising consultancy market.

Over the years experience has shown that, at least in East Africa, networks did not really come to function in a manner that the original ideology had anticipated. There were problems in the scope as well as in the actual nature of interaction. The scope remained rather limited in that researchers had great difficulties in communicating, let alone sharing, with policy makers and practitioners. In terms of the nature of interacting, there emerged little that could be termed networking as there were very few mutual flows: the nodal points hardly operated as such, while in the periphery contact points have tended to wait for goodies to flow their way without being much concerned about reciprocity.

It is easy to argue that educational networks, at least in East Africa, have tended to reflect the poverty of their institutional environment. In this view, researchers could not move because their institutions had no resources. Policy makers and practitioners were too busy keeping their professional, and their private, heads above water to be much concerned about collaboration for the sake of national education development. Sharing information is not popular in times of poverty as these bits of knowledge represent scarce capital that is often considered essential for personal advancement.

To be sure, in some countries there is a tendency to fragment the research community into ever smaller units, each putting up high-sounding names as antennae for capturing (external) resources that are available. Thus, if anything, networking and sharing appear to become more and more difficult. Yet, it also appears that in some African countries at least, networking among institutions or among groups of researchers works better than the same among individuals. This seems not so much dependent on resources as on clear agreements reached within and among those organizations concerning who is responsible for what and how these responsibilities are carried out. Beyond this it depends very much on the nature of leadership and management in the organization.

There is also the influence of donor agencies that should not be discounted. Agencies have a habit of setting the tone by making it very clear by whom and how they would want local research or consultancy work to be done. Their favorites are individuals, and rarely is there an effort to approach organizations and ask them to come with proposals that relate to their interests and modes of operation. Organizations or institutions, along with their capacity development, seem in practice to be systematically ignored. This has a bearing on relations between individual researchers, and their willingness to cooperate within organizational frameworks and to share information.

Thus there may be a fairly complex relationship between the strength of the state and higher education institutions and the quality of networking. Where it was thought at one time that the latter can prosper as the first gets weaker, we have at least come to realize that networking is highly dependent on institutional tolerance if not outright support. But in the African situation it may be the very idea of networks of individuals being quite separate from their institutions that needs to be overhauled. Progress may be made if there is greater acknowledgement of the institutions, organizations, or groups as potential networks themselves and that the quality of networking in the wider professional context would be strongly influenced by the realization of that potential.

NETWORKING, RESTRICTION OF INFORMATION, AND DEMOCRATIZATION IN AFRICA

Katherine Namuddu

A great deal of moral support has been given to a variety of African institutions and scholars over the past two decades so as to encourage them to set up networks. Donors have also put in money to support the work of such networks in disseminating research on education. Unfortunately, these experiences and their outcomes generally have been disappointing to those inside and outside the continent who had looked upon networking as an important process in removing the barriers of poor communication characteristic of African intellectual efforts.

The factors listed as important constraints to functional networking include (1) lack of funds, (2) a small research capacity and overworked academicians and scholars, and (3) absence of a basic supportive infrastructure for communication. But it is generally recognized that communication, even among staff in the same department, is often less than satisfactory. Why do networks have such a hard time functioning in Africa?

Functional networking must be undergirded by an intellectual culture and environment that has at least three characteristics. First, the potential participants should believe that while information garnered through research and other disciplined methods of inquiry should always be as accurate as possible in order to form a good foundation for future work, it need not be phenomenally accurate in order for it to be communicated to others. In other words, it is accepted that all knowledge and information is imperfect, and therefore, amenable to improvement by anyone with the skills to do so.

Second, the potential participants should make a distinction between the status of those who generate information and the status of the information itself. Important people do not necessarily generate important information, and ordinary people do originate useful information. Third, the potential participants should believe that they have something worth sharing with others. It is a belief in these three factors which encourages the formation of communities of scholars with a primary commitment to the growth of knowledge rather than the advancement of an individual.

But a commitment to these three beliefs which embody the fundamental goal for the creation, evolution, and growth of any functional network, is something which is generally missing within the majority of African intellectual institutions and environments. Scholars do not believe that the process of perfecting information is ultimately a collective and community responsibility rather than the preserve of an individual. As a result researchers want to generate perfect information and, therefore, usually spend a long time working on it, often in secret. The community of scholars in a particular field of study or activity is deprived of an opportunity to interact with the information by reading it, subjecting it to criticism, commenting on its validity and utility, and referring to it in their own works. Moreover, scholars often use the social status of authors in order to place value on the information.

Overall, few functional networks have developed in Africa because of a number of constraints, of which the most obvious are, first, intellectual environments do not always support and nurture the three processes which are intimately linked to the growth of a community of scholars, namely: research and inquiry; communication of knowledge through a variety of media and fora; and open criticism of whatever knowledge is available.

Second, increasing modernization and the infusion of external ideas and practices have not really replaced factors such as age and social status which were and continue to be used to restrict the generation and dissemination of information in traditional and closed societies.

Third, a new set of social factors based on either political patronage or competition for scarce resources are used to diminish the importance of information generated by those people who do not possess or have access to the trimmings of these kinds of social power and authority.

Finally, donors who are used to the smooth operation of basically informal networks among communities of scholars in the industrialized world have attempted to entice African scholars to create institutionalized networks. This has been done without first understanding that the absence of locally initiated and sustained communication is in itself the most important evidence that the necessary community structures and beliefs needed to support functional networks have yet to emerge from within Africa.

It has recently been argued that the democratization processes underway in Africa are likely to encourage the emergence and proper functioning of networks. It is asserted that democratization, by enabling the emergence of a variety of voices, will result in the generation of many different kinds of information that is needed by various groups and constituencies, and that will have to be communicated through a variety of fora including networks. This scenario may, however, take a long time to emerge because of three factors.

First, the process of democratization itself promises to be long, socially divisive, and tortuous, and will therefore likely encourage the emergence of cliques who have a desire to restrict the flow of information.

Second, despite the wide variety of political rhetoric on the landscape claiming to represent different voices, it is only a small segment of society that is involved in genuine democratization. Third, the activities of the few functional networks which have been in continuous existence for some years are still donor driven, so that their participants have not yet managed to create a locally supported rationale for their existence, including the development of democratic mechanisms for expanding the network within particular countries or institutions.

THE CULTURE OF NETWORKING
IN EDUCATIONAL RESEARCH IN
EASTERN AND SOUTHERN AFRICA

Lydia Nyati-Ramahobo

The Educational Research Network in Eastern and Southern Africa (ERNESA) was founded in 1985 with the purpose of building and sustaining a vibrant community of educational researchers, policy makers, and practitioners. This aim could only be achieved through networking. Researchers in the region needed to network among themselves, and so did policy makers and practitioners. More importantly, the three groups needed to network more effectively with each other as they shared common goals of improving the quality of life in their respective countries. A culture of networking and sharing therefore, needed to be cultivated, nurtured, and sustained.

This chapter discusses the nature of networking within the region and highlights factors which affect the creation of a networking culture within ERNESA countries and between ERNESA and other networks with specific reference to educational research. The reasons for networking, how it is done, and the factors affecting it form the overall culture of networking in educational research in the region. This chapter argues that the similarities and differences in political, economic, and educational conditions within the membership of ERNESA serve as key ingredients for enrichment in the creation of a strong culture of networking and sharing.

THE NATURE AND NEED FOR NETWORKING

Networking is characteristic of human behavior. It is a way of life. People network at various levels in order to achieve different goals. At the village level, communities form clusters which work together in the fields to remove weeds as one person cannot do it alone in their own field. Small communities come together to build schools at central places for their children and governments come together to fight common enemies such as hunger, war, and disease. In order to facilitate a healthy networking relationship, all parties must share common experiences resulting in common problems yielding a natural need to network. All parties must perceive the problem as a priority in order to have equal commitment. There must be obvious benefits from the networking relationship for all parties and each party must be willing to give before it takes. Each party must possess a unique characteristic to contribute to the relationship; this will provide diversity which will facilitate the need to network. The idea is to pull resources together for the benefit of all members involved. It is characterized by sharing to meet a common need. Networking is catalytic to development as it provides for cross fertilization of ideas for better productivity.

Isolation has always been perceived as an undesirable element in human behavior. People who do not interact are negatively viewed by society and they usually remain uninformed, inactive, and ineffective. Networking is therefore the norm rather than the exception.

Within the eastern and southern African regions, isolation of educational researchers from one another, and from policy makers and practitioners, was identified as a major setback to the development of educational research in the region (Komba, 1990). This isolation led to duplication of efforts in the midst of scarce resources and more importantly was counterproductive for achievement of the goal of educational research to inform policy planning and practice. The isolation also led to lack of sharing of the skills necessary for the generation of information needed by policy makers and practitioners. It built walls which blocked the flow of information within countries and between countries. Channels of communication were nonexistent hence the need to build them through networking. ERNESA countries are therefore networking for four main goals: (1) capacity building through training, (2) carrying out research, (3) bridging the gap between researchers and policy makers, and (4) dissemination of research information throughout the region.

THE STRUCTURE OF NETWORKING

The network is made up of twelve countries with national associations headed by chairpersons. The chairpersons make up the council, the highest decision-making body. The council meets once a year to formulate policies and share experiences of the individual associations, fostering the networking relationship between associations. One of the councillors is elected as chairperson of the network. The secretariat is the executive administrative body, implementing the decisions of council. It is the pivot of the network, facilitating the flow of information within the network. It is the overall coordinating body, nurturing the functional networking relationship between individual associations and balancing national with regional needs. The chairperson of the network connects the secretariat to the council and the secretariat connects the entire network to other external networks.

The twelve countries are further grouped into three subregional networks based on geographical grounds as follows: Botswana, Lesotho, and Swaziland Educational Research Association (BOLESWA); Central African Educational Research Association (CAERA) for Malawi, Mozambique, Zambia, and Zimbabwe; and Kenya, Uganda, Tanzania Educational Research Association (KUTERA). Negotiations are taking place to situate two members of the network, namely, Namibia and Ethiopia, in the relevant subnetworks. The subnetworks are coordinated by subregional coordinators working closely with chairpersons of national associations in the respective countries.

At the national level, individual associations network with ministries of education and other educational institutions from which they attract membership including policy makers, teachers, education officers, and other personnel. It also builds relationships with donor agencies. It is the national association which is responsible for capacity building at the grassroots level. It shares its activities and outputs with other networks in the subregion and through the secretariat such information is shared with the rest of the network. The national association has the responsibility to support itself and contribute to the running of the entire network through the secretariat. The strength of ERNESA lies, therefore, in its national associations serving as the organs of action.

This structure is congruent with networking systems within the African tradition in which the individual is not only part of the nuclear family but the extended family and the community at large. For instance, in most sub-Saharan African cultures, a wedding is first announced to the immediate family, then to members of the extended family, and finally everyone is welcome and involved. The administrative structure is also consistent with the chieftainship structure in which communities within a village have subchiefs or headmen who directly report to the chief, and the chief communicates with people through subchiefs. A visitor to the village is reported to the chief who will welcome him or her and introduce him or her to the subchiefs and the people. The structure is a democratic one, allowing for autonomy, flexibility, easy flow of information, and, more importantly, it is not externally imposed but it is part and parcel of the African tradition.

FACTORS AFFECTING NETWORKING WITHIN ERNESA COUNTRIES

ERNESA countries have certain characteristics which could either facilitate or threaten the sustainability of the network. Political, economic, and cultural factors are explored to speculate on their impact on the vulnerability of the network. Issues of fairness, commitment, and access are crucial to any networking relationship. Is everyone getting a fair deal and are all equally committed to the common goal? Are channels of communication open and functional providing the necessary information to everyone at all times? Is the relationship supported by other relationships, in other words, is cooperation manifested in more than one common bond and experience? In any networking relationship, negative answers to these questions could render the network vulnerable.

Political Factors

Most countries in the network have common colonial experiences which have influenced their education systems and sociocultural conditions. Nine ERNESA countries were former British colonies; two (Tanzania, later British, and Namibia) were German colonies; one (Mozambique) was a Portuguese colony and one (Ethiopia) was an Italian colony. Five ERNESA countries are now democracies, namely, Botswana, Zambia, Zimbabwe, Ethiopia, and Namibia. Two are kingdoms: Lesotho and Swaziland. Three are "one party but moving towards uncertain democracy" (Peresuh, 1993): Tanzania, Mozambique, and Malawi. Common political problems have resulted in political networks, for instance, five ERNESA countries are members of the Frontline States whose responsibility is to assist liberation movements in the southern region, especially those who fought against apartheid. These are Botswana, Zambia, Zimbabwe, Mozambique, and Tanzania. In East Africa the East African Community (EAC) network worked for sometime but was later abandoned. These political ties have facilitated networking relationships in education as will be elaborated later.

One notes that as the political climates in some countries change for the better, educational research networking relationships are facilitated. This is the case with Namibia which became a member of the network after independence. In Ethiopia a functional association was formed after the civil war ended. In Mozambique and Malawi the move towards democracy, even though not completely achieved, has facilitated the establishment of research associations and the interaction of researchers with other ERNESA countries has been enhanced. As the political situation improves, positive signs to develop ties with South Africa are showing. For instance, South Africa is already a participant in the ERNESA Africa Policy Dialogue Project. Thoughts to incorporate Eritrea are present within the network.

It is mainly due to unfavorable political climates that ERNESA has not been able to attract all countries in the region to the network. Angola, in its delicate state of democracy and Somalia in its delicate state of uncertain future have no ties at all, even at the informal level, with the network. Likewise, Rwanda and Burundi are not part of the network.

Political climates also determine the base for each national association in each country. In Botswana, Lesotho, Swaziland, Namibia, Zimbabwe, Zambia, Kenya, and Uganda, national associations are based at universities because the political climates in these countries are tolerant to autonomous networking. On the other hand, in Mozambique, Tanzania, and Malawi (until recently), national associations are based within the Ministry of Education due to the uncertain democratic state of the country where governments want to monitor external relations.

Economic Factors

ERNESA countries are relatively poor with varying degrees of poverty. They are dependent on either minerals or agriculture as the backbone of their economies and also on foreign aid. Countries in the south especially Botswana, Lesotho, and Swaziland (the BOLESWA countries) are dependent on South Africa for goods and services including food. These countries together with South Africa are members of a Customs Union, which allows nearly free movement of goods and services within the countries. Nine ERNESA countries are members of Southern Africa

Development Community (SADC), which was formed in 1980 to reduce dependency on South Africa and increase trade among themselves. These are: Botswana, Lesotho, Swaziland, Zambia, Zimbabwe, Mozambique, Tanzania, Malawi, and Namibia. Six ERNESA countries are members of the Preferential Trade Area (PTA) network: Ethiopia, Uganda, Kenya, Tanzania, Malawi, and Zambia. This network encourages intertrade as one country produces goods and services needed by the others.

Thus both political and economic ties are well established within the region and hence cooperation within the subregional networks of ERNESA are supported by more than one thread.

Educational Factors

As ERNESA countries belong to the same region they have common colonial experiences which have influenced their education policies and sociocultural conditions.

During the precolonial period, education emphasized traditional values of manhood and motherhood. Young male adults were trained to become good men, warriors, and husbands while young female adults were trained to become good wives and mothers. This type of education emphasized respect, loyalty, and diligence.

Western education was introduced to Africa by missionaries during the colonial period. This type of education replaced traditional education which was considered "pagan" (Shaw, 1989) or "heathen" (Parsons, 1983). Colonial education was meant to "civilize" Africans, to replace traditional customs with Western ways of life. The syllabus emphasized religion and language, and so education became closely associated with Christianity, Western civilization and elitism (Shaw, 1989). Toward independence, education prepared white collar workers to man the postcolonial states. Practical education was less emphasized (Parsons,1983) while excellence in the language of the colonial powers was required.

After independence education policies within the region experienced a shift from colonial education to education to meet the immediate needs of the society. The trend towards secular education, de-emphasizing religion and practical skills and emphasizing English, French, and Portuguese, continued to produce white collar workers. Education was seen as a crucial aspect of economic and human resource development, hence the emphasis on postprimary education during the early years of independence (Ministry of Education and Culture, Republic of Malawi, 1985). Current education policies seek to provide universal primary and adult education and eliminate illiteracy (Republic of Botswana, 1977). Education is also seen as an important aspect of liberation from colonial dominance of any form hence the need for the young and the old to be educated in order to understand the changing world around them. The role of culture is seen as important in this regard and efforts to inject it into school syllabuses are emphasized (Castles et al., 1981). Implementation of these policies has met a number of problems, especially financial problems, calling for international aid and networking among the concerned countries.

Currently, ERNESA countries have common educational concerns, such as the provision of education to all citizens, teenage pregnancy, environmental education, health education, curriculum relevancy, and teacher education, to mention a few. All ERNESA countries are aspiring to create democratic environments conducive to sustainable development, leading to self-reliance and unity. This goal has been realized to varying degrees by different countries but the commitment of each country to these ideals are undoubted. All ERNESA countries are committed to the development of education as an investment in the future. These common goals and problems could be addressed through networking mechanisms in which countries share experiences of working solutions.

Within the region, countries in the subregional clusters mentioned earlier (BOLESWA, CAERA, and KUTERA) developed an infrastructure in higher education in the 1970s. The three countries in each subregion joined together to form one university, the University of Botswana, Lesotho, and Swaziland, the University of Rhodesia and Nyasaland, and the University of East Africa respectively. Currently, the countries have developed their independent universities but cooperation in training and material development and other areas has continued. The BOLESWA biennial educational research symposium has facilitated the interaction of educators and educational researchers not only in the subregion but in the whole region hence creating potential for a sustainable community in which the culture of sharing and interaction could be the norm.

NETWORKING WITH OTHER NETWORKS

More than a dozen educational networks exist within the eastern and southern African region (Komba, 1992). Some have common goals, others have slightly different foci. The number of networks is increasing and "there is obvious need for the creation of a regional network forum to sort out who is doing what for which purpose" (Kinunda, 1991, quoted in Komba, 1992, p. 12). The mushrooming of networks should be viewed as a positive development for it fosters not only the culture of networking but competitiveness. Only those networks which can compete will survive and this is a challenge for those networks which share the same objectives. Competition could yield a healthy atmosphere for with it will come productivity, creativity, and better quality. Such an atmosphere is not only desirable to the region but to donors for they will put their money where they expect the best results. More networks in educational research will specifically accelerate capacity building in the form of more and better expertise and research findings, and hence improve the quality of life.

Of major concern, however, is the lack of networking among most networks. It is necessary for networks, especially those with common goals to define their working relationships so as to maintain harmony and foster the culture of sharing. Networking among networks is also necessary for the utilization of limited resources in the region. Another concern is that the proliferation of networks might spread the limited available resources (human and material) too thinly to have an impact on development, hence the creation of more networks for the sake of competition may prove detrimental to development.

ERNESA has an open networking policy and has networked on a number of projects with other networks, with whom they have had shared goals, both inside and outside the region and with donor agencies. Clear examples are projects such as ERNESA, African Women Development and Communication Network (FEM-NET) and United Nations Children's Fund (UNICEF) with respect to "Girl Child," and the ERNESA-Harvard and Educational Research Network of Tanzania (ERNETA)-NORRAG projects on the policy analysis. Lessons have been learned from these relationships, but more importantly, the mere existence of the relationships is indicative of the development of a culture of networking within the region.

Challenges for the Future

A culture of networking is gradually developing within the region not only in educational research but in other areas. However, in order to further develop and sustain a community of researchers, policy makers, and practitioners, a strengthening of the activities of educational research networks within ERNESA is necessary. As education is a political, economic, and cultural endeavor, economic, political, and cultural bonds that exist between the countries do facilitate the education bond but they do not necessarily guarantee it. However, when countries network in more than one area, the opportunities for new relationships to be established and sustained are improved and therefore more networking relationships should be encouraged within ERNESA countries.

For ERNESA to sustain itself, all national networks need to be committed to the goals of the network. This commitment should be felt at the individual, national, subregional, and regional levels. The commitment of individual researchers and policy makers is critical if the objectives of their national networks and those of the regional network are to be upheld. Commitment could be sustained if the regional network has something to offer to its member associations and ERNESA has great potential in this regard.

There is also the need to develop and strengthen other networking mechanisms such as library exchange among universities, attachments (individual scholars and students), collaborative research projects, training schemes, e-mail, newsletters, journals, and bulletins. This will not only foster the culture of networking in the region but provide opportunities for research to reach and benefit all stakeholders in education.

CONCLUSIONS

Despite problems of self-centeredness, loss of legitimacy, excessive formalization of the network, failure to properly utilize diversity, poor communication systems, oversensitive political environments, poor economies, and others (Komba, 1992), ERNESA has cultivated a culture of networking in the region which has a potential for further development. A few of the weaker dividing walls have been broken, small bridges built, and a foundation for better communication channels laid. The diversity of the membership of ERNESA serves as an essential ingredient for the need to share and learn from one another. The differences in political ideologies and economic capabilities should not necessarily be issues that divide ERNESA as they can be issues that bind it.

PROBLEMS OF NETWORKING: THE ERNESA EXPERIENCE

Donatus Komba

As a research network ERNESA has been and continues to be affected adversely by whatever general problems normally impede the development and/or utilization of research capacity in eastern and southern Africa. These include, for example, the low status conventionally accorded to local research and researchers; underfunding of local research; over-sensitivity of governments to the critical nature of research in general; poor communication infrastructure within and across countries of the region; the lack of research training and retraining facilities; presence of cutthroat competition among local researchers for meager funds which limits sharing and collaboration among them; the stagnation and even decline of our fragile economies, and so on.

Besides these problems there are others that have to do with the very essence and raison d'être of the ERNESA network. The first one has been the temptation of members to equate networking simply with the creation of national research associations which become members of ERNESA as a regional body. While admittedly the formation and/or strengthening of national research associations has been a difficult and commendable task, it is true that it is the process of information sharing and collaborative activities which make a network a network. Associations should be taken as nothing but facilitating contexts for networking purposes. In this regard ERNESA has yet to fully move into the process mode of networking and become an information and activity network.

The second problem has to do with the temptation for the network to become regional without having national or local legitimacy. It should be noted in this regard that from its inception ERNESA believed that its strength lay in the development, strengthening, and operation of national research associations supported by such regional training schemes as KUTERA and BOLESWA. That is why for not less than two years (1986–88) it did only that. But since then there has been pressure arising from our own expectations and those of well-wishers and supporters that we should quickly evolve tangible and plausible regional level activities. As a consequence, there is now a real danger that the regional action plan we are working on may not represent common ground or intersection of action plans agreed upon and undertaken at national level. If this happens then ERNESA may lose its local grip and with it its legitimacy and strength.

The third problem has to do with the development of shortsighted aims if ERNESA is tempted to settle with encouraging networking among researchers and research organizations or institutions while its farsighted goal was to ensure that research reached out of the shelves and universities and informed policy makers and practitioners. More precisely, the aim ultimately was to ensure that research became part and parcel of education policy making practice. ERNESA has hardly begun to move closer to that ultimate goal. The ERNESA-Harvard collaboration[1] and to some extent the ERNETA-NORRAG project are but humble beginnings in that direction.

The fourth problem has to do with striking a balance between institutionalization of the network and personalization of the network. Admittedly, networks are strengthened by their power to enable individuals to surmount the institutional barriers to the generation and free flow of ideas and information, creativity, and openness. Yet networks have to exist in a world where government and even donor and other agencies are not used to working with entities which don't bear an institutional stamp, which is often the case with networks. In these circumstances networks have to institutionalize and formalize themselves, and in the process there is the danger of them losing the life and strength they draw from individual touch and networking charisma of their members. At the same time, institutionalizing may guard against personalization of networks and initiate more systematic procedures of changing leadership and organization. There is thus a give-and-take that requires careful balancing in this regard.

The fifth problem has to do with the disturbing tendency of donor and development agencies to support capacity-building schemes in a manner that bypasses and renders irrelevant existing research networks in the region. This is sometimes justified by their fear that networks in their current stage may not deliver goods as expected from institutions. It seems for them results are more important than the process that networking is all about. With time it is becoming difficult to get anyone to support the process as something worthwhile. One can detect a tendency among ourselves to hive off training schemes and treat them as separate networks although initially they were started as part and parcel of ERNESA.

The sixth problem for ERNESA has been the instability of the network as it has been trying to make a transition towards institutionalizing itself through registration in Botswana. For the last two years IDRC has been trying to wean ERNESA into independence by a joint coordination from Botswana and from Dar Es Salaam. This has been difficult because of soaring communication costs.

NOTE

1. BRIDGES, the Basic Research and Implementation in Developing Education Systems Project, was financed by USAID and directed by the Harvard Institute for International

Development. The project participated with ERNESA in the planning and carrying out of a seminar on research findings and requirements for countries in southern Africa. The seminar brought together ministry policy makers and education researchers.

THE AFRICAN EDUCATIONAL RESEARCH NETWORK: PROGRESS AND PROSPECTS AT MID-DECADE

Milton E. Ploghoft

The African Educational Research Network (AERN) was formally established in 1992 at a meeting of representatives of universities that had cooperated in various ways in African educational development for several decades. Clark Atlanta University was host to this organizational and planning meeting, held in the new International Program Center there. The founding institutions were Bayero University in Kano, Nigeria, the University of Manchester in the United Kingdom, the National University of Lesotho, Kenyatta University in Nairobi, Oklahoma State University, the University of Ottawa, Clark Atlanta University, and Ohio University. Dr. Shelby Lewis, associate vice president for research and director of International Programs at Clark Atlanta University, was elected as the first chairperson of the AERN. Dr. Milton E. Ploghoft, professor emeritus and former director of the Center for Higher Education was selected to serve as coordinator. North Carolina State University at Raleigh, Addis Ababa University, the University of Zimbabwe, and Makerere University in Uganda became members of the AERN in 1994.

The AERN was not the product of sudden inspiration on the part of any single individual. It was created because earlier commitments of individuals and institutions to technical assistance projects, consultancies, and contracted services supported by one donor agency or another had evolved into greater, although less formal, commitments to share the rich resources and services these universities and their scholars have to offer. The network was seen as a vehicle that would enable cooperating universities to maintain regular communication and to focus energies and activities upon selected aspects of African educational development. Agendas for action would be developed and pursued.

In 1985, Ohio University president Charles J. Ping had urged that universities avoid the "contract mentality" which devalues continuing relationships among universities once the funded project has been concluded. President Ping called for the "sharing of the richness that is the university" through means beyond traditional grants and contracts. The AERN endorsed this spirit of sharing which should benefit all members.

The early experiences of the AERN indicate that the efforts of individual professors to share the richness of their universities through collaborations with like-minded professors and administrators at other universities have been supported at departmental, college, and university levels by modest, in-kind contributions and praise. The contract mentality seems to be alive and well in most universities while sharing the richness of the university through unfunded collaborations is not attractive to departments who must direct their attention and resources to concerns such as promotion, tenure, and salary increases. The strong commitments of a few persons in each university were essential.

With one or two notable exceptions, the AERN has progressed slowly but steadily toward its goals because of such commitment and effort by university representatives who have attained senior status as administrators and professors, hence able to move beyond the constraints of academic bureaucracies and competing agendas. It has not been uncommon for AERN executive committee members to personally defray the costs associated with attending planning conferences, seminars, and committee sessions. The contributions individuals have made to support the AERN through its infancy period amount to thousands of dollars.

This information should not be interpreted as a testimonial to sacrifices made by the founders of the AERN nor as harsh criticism of universities whose laudable intentions, publicly proclaimed, fall short of actualization. The member universities have provided basic support for clerical and communication costs of participation in the AERN. The representatives have been given time to attend network functions. Many vice chancellors, presidents, and deans have given freely of their time and expertise to consider AERN goals and activities and to represent AERN to other agencies and organizations. Financial support for symposia and for stipends for graduate assistantships has been provided. Development officers and senior administrators have given freely of their time to prepare, submit, and follow up the requests for funding of specific AERN activities.

The status and qualifications of the persons who undertook to create such an association is, of course, very critical to survival and success, and will continue to be so. However, the increasing participation and assumption of leadership roles by the major stakeholders, the African graduate students, may very well turn out to be the most critical success element in the AERN experience over the long run.

Education leaders at university and government levels in eastern and southern Africa had provided helpful working models through organizations such as ERNESA, BOLESWA, and KUTERA (Eshiwani, 1991). Networking there has strengthened and extended the community of scholars that can be involved in setting research agendas, sharing expertise, and disseminating findings to ministries and agencies at national levels. This is the sort of networking that Eshiwani saw as "perhaps the savior" for scholars who live and work in a continent "where researchers are isolated, resources are meager and the problems to be solved, frightening" (Eshiwani, 1991, p. 3). Recognition of the need to extend communication among educators who were concerned with African educational development and the urgency of bringing into this circle the thousands of African graduate students at overseas universities grew out of Ohio's African Educational Research Symposia.

The African Educational Research Symposia, first offered by Ohio University's Center for Higher Education in 1985, were inspired by the earlier observations of Keetla Masogo in which he called upon the universities of the North to provide more and better opportunities for African graduate students to conduct research projects that were relevant to the development agendas back home. Masogo suggested that African education leaders in universities and ministries be invited to participate in the research development of the African graduate students who pursue degree studies in overseas institutions. In an attempt to increase the exchanges of information among African students concerned with educational research, the Ohio symposium was conceived. Vice chancellors, deans, permanent secretaries, and professors from universities in Lesotho, Swaziland, Botswana, Canada, and the United Kingdom were very much involved as planners and presenters in the symposia of the mid-1980s in Ohio.

The same kind of collaborations characterized the biennial symposia that have been sponsored by educational research associations of the BOLESWA nations since 1987. The BOLESWA symposia now attract educators from many nations beyond those nations and that region. Ohio University marked its tenth year of sponsorship of the symposia in 1995 when more than ninety graduate students from twenty universities and twenty-three nations participated. The University of Botswana and BERA hosted the fifth biennial research symposium in August of 1995.

Energy and foresight were provided at the outset by seasoned educators from all sides, including Vice Chancellor Lydia Makhubu and Permanent Secretary Nsibande from Swaziland, Vice Chancellor Tom Tlou from Botswana, professors Colin Mackay of Canada, John Turner from Manchester, Kenneth King from Edinburgh, Dr. Shelby Lewis from Clark Atlanta University, and Ambassador Cynthia Shepherd Perry (Sierra Leone and Burundi). The momentum that was created was without doubt responsible for the continuing success of the symposia and inspired the efforts to regularize institutional relationships and to identify the purposes and directions through an association that would one day become the African Educational Research Network.

Three aspects of African educational development that have moved the AERN to its current emphasis upon electronic information exchange as one means to building individual and institutional capacities are the widely recognized isolation of African scholars, the great potential of the rich but underdeveloped human resources that are to be found in the thousands of African graduate students who study in overseas universities, and the rapidly declining resources of the libraries of African universities.

The isolation of professors cited by Eshiwani was elaborated upon in the report, *A Consultation on Higher Education in Africa* by Trevor Coombe. The most commonly expressed concern of vice chancellors was for increased contacts of their faculties with colleagues in other universities, both within and outside their respective nations. The emergence of a community of African scholars is essential to the future of African universities, in the view of Coombe, and he stated that effective and efficient means of communication is a prerequisite to the emergence of such a community (Coombe, 1991). The isolation problem is further exacerbated by the sharp decline in the research-supporting capacities of African universities which have been reported by Kinyanjui to approach 50 percent in the past decade (Kinyanjui, 1990). Odedra-Straub (1992) has observed that 90 percent of the information about Africa lies in databases in the West, concluding that the communication/information problem was the most manifest of all barriers to capacity building in African universities.

Odedra-Straub's conclusion has been validated by the studies of the Sub-Saharan Libraries Project of the American Association for the Advancement of Science (AAAS). Levey (1993), director of the AAAS studies, has reported that the rising costs of subscriptions and shipping costs have contributed to sharp declines in the periodical holdings that are essential to both instruction and research activity in African universities. Makerere University reports that the number of periodical subscriptions has fallen from about 800 in 1983 to 200 in 1995. The AAAS has launched efforts to moderate the information crisis through the use of databases and text materials that may be made available on CD-ROM and has been exploring the feasibility of utilizing other information technologies in this regard.

The AERN was further encouraged to consider an electronic information exchange project by the spread, over the past five to seven years, of computer networking across Africa. RINAF, the Regional Information Network for Africa, has been active in developing and disseminating information regarding the use of telecommunications technologies within and among the nations of Africa. Bellman and Tindumbon (1991) report that a study conducted in 1990 found that virtually all of the modern information technologies are in use in some African institutions. They estimated that close to 10,000 computers were in use in business, education, government, and NGOs in Kenya alone, a figure that is surely out of date now, thanks to the efforts of Ochuodho and others at the African Regional Computer Centre in Nairobi.

The member universities of the AERN recognize the hurdles that must be overcome as they move to implement library collaborations using electronic information technologies to moderate the deficits in databases, references, periodicals, and other resources that are essential to high-quality teaching and research activity in modern universities. An important first step has been taken by all but one of the African members of AERN in the establishment of connectivity to the Internet through one of several nodes.

Kenyatta University, the University of Zimbabwe, the National University of Lesotho, Makerere University, and Addis Ababa University maintain connectivity and are prepared to move ahead with the technical assessments of hardware and software resources necessary to engage in library collaborations with their African and Northern partners. Northern members of the AERN are on-line but in the interest of candid reporting, the utilization of the "new" information technologies is far from universal among the faculties. As one might expect, the humanities, social sciences, and arts seem to lag behind the fields of mathematics, engineering, and the hard sciences in this respect. Fortunately, the libraries have built expertise and physical resources that are a prerequisite to collaborations that utilize these technologies.

While progress has been less rapid than desired, the development of both the library collaborations and the electronic research roundtables has been supported by the full participation of qualified individuals from African and Northern universities alike. The participation of Clifford Odaet of Makerere was made possible as a fringe benefit of his Fulbright Research Fellowship at Ohio University in 1994–95 and the continuing contributions of Visiting Professor Lazarus Jaji of the University of Zimbabwe began in the fall of 1993. Odaet and Jaji have provided critical links between their universities and the AERN and the Ohio University Libraries in the process of designing the library collaborations.

An AERN listserv was created in 1994 by Sofus Simonsen at North Carolina State to enhance communications among members and to provide a means for interested persons to learn about the network. It has provided a model after which a research roundtable listserv was to be later created.

The electronic research roundtables have attracted considerable attention and interest from African graduate students across the United States. Much of this contact has come through participation in the annual African Educational Research Symposia and from acquaintances among students from various nations. More than fifty African graduate students and many professors from African and Northern universities are now subscribers to a roundtable listserv that was established in April of 1995 by Kwabena Ofori-Attah, a doctoral candidate from Ghana. Justina Mbugua, doctoral candidate from Kenya and Chris Busang, a graduate student and media specialist from Botswana complete this core team of African educators who have led the development of research roundtables.

The *Journal of Practice in Development Education* is edited by John Turner at the University of Manchester and is the official journal of the AERN. An AERN newsletter is published annually at Ohio University.

The advisory group of the AERN is comprised of specialists from various areas of education and computer mediated communications applications. Members of this group are Mayuri Odedra-Straub of Leonberg, Germany, an author and researcher in computer networking in African development; Lydia Nyati-Rama-hobo, professor at the University of Botswana and chair of ERNESA; Richard Chowning, professor at Abilene Christian University and head of the Technology Section for the African Studies Association; Juergen Hess, professor at Max Planck Institute in Berlin; Dr. Shelby Lewis, academic vice president at Morris Brown College in Atlanta, Georgia; and M. Michel Perdreau of Athens, Ohio, an international consultant in computer-mediated applications.

The AERN represents a voluntary association of universities that are committed to capacity building in areas of African educational research in all members of the AERN. There are no fees. Members support the costs of their participation and there are no salaried positions within the administration of the network. An executive committee representing the several universities determines policy, programs, and priorities. Membership is by invitation upon the recommendation of the executive committee. The current chair person of the AERN is Clifford Odaet. He will remain as chair until June 30, 1997.

Events over time will determine the nature and longevity of the AERN and its contributions, if any, to African educational development through applications of electronic information technology. It appears inevitable that the sharing of rich resources among the universities of Africa and the North will become much less expensive and far more accessible to the students and professors of the twenty-first century, as the advent and application of this technology moderate dependency upon the expensive transport of human and material resources around the earth.

Milton E. Ploghoft, professor emeritus at Ohio University, has filled the position of coordinator since the founding of the AERN. Additional information may be obtained by writing to the AERN Coordinator, Ohio University Libraries, Ohio University, Athens, Ohio, 45701; fax at (614) 592-5958; e-mail address ploghoft@ouvaxa.cats.ohiou.edu.

NETWORKING IN WEST AFRICA

William Rideout, Jr., and Richard Gilbert

Modern, albeit Western, science and technology began to enter into Africa in the form of colonial science which represented the structure and style of institutions in the ruling nations and, consequently, colonial societies remained dependent upon them for a long time. For some African nations, this dependence remains today.

The situation changed in some societies with the advent of political freedom soon after the end of the Second World War and the beginning of the new international political and economic order. Some African leaders gave priority to building scientific and technological infrastructures, such as universities, as necessary preconditions to social and economic development. These efforts have been, and to a larger extent still are, beset with many problems peculiar to these developing regions.

One of the main problems in Africa's research can be characterized as a linkage problem. For instance, the problems entail coordinating the total research effort to meet national goals; linking education to research, and both of them to production and services to meet basic human needs; finding the right mix of long-term basic research and short-term developmental work directly related to solving immediate practical problems; combining universal criteria of scientific excellence with the necessities of doing relevant science in the national context; and finding a compromise between strong antiscientific traditions and subcultures with modernity and scientific ethos to the extent possible without causing total chaos. The Educational Research Network for Western and Central Africa (ERNWACA) provides an example of an effort to coordinate research efforts and concentrate resources on specified areas of national and regional importance.

THE ERNWACA MODEL

Over the past decade there has been an impressive growth in educational research networking worldwide. In this context, two subregional networks have been created in Africa: the Educational Research Network in Eastern and Southern Africa (ERNESA) with subregional headquarters in Nairobi, Kenya, and, more recently, ERNWACA, which in French is Réseau Ouest et Central Africain de Recherche en Éducation (ROCARE). ERNWACA grew out of a meeting in Free-town, Sierra Leone, of several educational researchers and practitioners from the region which was sponsored by the International Development Research Centre (IDRC) early in 1989 to review the state of educational research in the subregion. Near the end of 1989, after several months of continuing deliberations, a two-year network development project, designated as ERNWACA's first phase, was initiated and funded by IDRC.

Since 1989 there has been growing concern with promoting greater coopera-tion/collaboration within ERNWACA and between ERNWACA and other networks in the African region. This would enhance relationships between ERNESA and ERNWACA and perhaps promote the establishment of a network for the Portu-guese-speaking nations since they do not, in effect, participate in either network. In addition, there has also been an emphasis on developing supraregional networks such as the Southern Educational Research Initiative (SERI) which seeks to promote South-South collaboration among educational researchers. In brief, SERI, as pro-posed in 1993, would focus on "research information sharing and research capacity building" among the subregional networks (Cheng, 1994, p. 1).

Administrative Structure and Organization

Initially ERNWACA had two coordinating offices, one in Togo for the francophone states and another in Ghana for the anglophone; each was led by a coordinator who was also a professor. They were responsible for promoting the creation of national network facilities in each of their constituencies and then for developing cross-na-tional linkages within and between the ERNWACA subregion. Participating member states were francophone Benin, Burkina Faso, Côte D'Ivoire, Mali, Senegal, and Togo, plus anglophone Gambia, Ghana, Nigeria, and Sierra Leone, and bilingual Cameroon. In 1994 francophone Guinea joined and while Zaire and Liberia both expressed interest, internal political crises have prevented their involvement.

During Phase I it became apparent that administratively dividing the subregion into francophone and anglophone components did not promote the collaboration and integration which ERNWACA sought to stimulate and achieve. Therefore, with the initiation of Phase II a major modification was to centralize the subregional office and have that Office of the Regional Coordinator staffed by personnel fully proficient in French and English as well as professionally qualified by both franco-phone and anglophone educational systems. The Malian Ministries of Basic and Higher Education, and Scientific Research supported the designation of the Supe-rior Institute for Training and Applied Research (ISFRA) as an appropriate location with facilities which could be made available to ERNWACA with free infrastructural support and amenities. Consequently, Bamako, Mali, was designated the site of the Office of the Regional Coordinator and Lalla Ben Barka, educated in France and the United States, professionally involved in development in the Third World, especially in Africa, and recipient of the UNESCO literacy prize in 1993, agreed to serve in that position.

Research Agenda

In each of the member states national networks led by national coordinators were to be set up and the initial tasks assigned were to prepare a state-of-the-art review of educational research supervised by a principal researcher in each country, to organize national seminars that would discuss the reviews (an inventory of indigenous national research), to identify national research priorities, and to contribute on a regular basis to a subregional network newsletter.

Regional research themes. While difficulties were experienced during this phase, the positive results derived from the members' state-of-the-art reviews provided a wealth of national research studies which highlighted key subregional priorities for further educational research. Based on these findings ERNWACA, at a meeting held in Senegal in January 1992, announced three regional research themes: (1) access to and retention in education in relation to community participation, (2) connection between education and society through enhanced participation of the community, and (3) contribution of nonformal education to the process of basic education for all.

Research missions. Phase II was officially launched in October 1993. Research programs were defined, support to national networks was offered, a framework for engaging in collaboration between member institutions was designed, and a procedure for sharing and exchanging ideas among researchers, decision makers, and donors was proposed. The operational objectives were proposed as four missions:

> Mission One: to consolidate the ERNWACA network on the regional and national levels by reinforcing communications systems, setting up mechanisms of quality control for research activities, establishing and using data banks, and publishing research results.
>
> Mission Two: to improve educational research capacity through training researchers in methodology, conducting refresher courses, and establishing an information network for the dissemination of research results.
>
> Mission Three: to establish contacts between English- and French-speaking researchers. The network's mission is to facilitate cooperation among researchers from member countries, develop exchanges in order to draw up transnational research topics, and conduct research with multinational multidisciplinary teams in order to facilitate comparative analysis.
>
> Mission Four: to develop a culture of research in the region. The network will aim to reinforce the concept of cooperation and voluntary service by

encouraging participation in research activities, and suing market techniques to disseminate research results to ensure their use.

Research topics. Of pervasive operational significance for ERNWACA's priority to reinforce collaboration among regional researchers through the exchange of information and experience, as well as through the implementation of common projects, was the agreement by national members to establish four research topics based on the three areas of research priority. Moreover, for each of the four topics at least two member states were to be involved and for each of the four there would be both francophone and anglophone states involved.

NATIONAL RESEARCH CENTERS

The locus of the national research centers' offices and those assigned to participate on the national teams vary from state to state. The Office of the Regional Coordinator, which since its creation has also participated in Guinea's admission to ERNWACA, is basically interested only in determining that there is adequate support including qualified personnel made available so the national office can fulfill its educational research obligations as defined by ERNWACA. Thus, the units within the national bureaucracy which provide the researchers are diverse. For example, at the ERNWACA meeting held in the Gambia in June 1994 to harmonize transnational research projects the largest number of national team members (twelve) were teachers, researchers, and administrators from tertiary level institutions, universities, and teacher training colleges, but with highly divergent foci, such as vocational and technical training, psychology, economics of education, planning, and evaluation. Those from national ministries and institutes were the second largest group and held positions in management, administration, planning, and youth and sports.

At other meetings, such as the once in Senegal in October 1994 for the purpose of studying research methodology, the number attending increased and included several from national pedagogical institutes in three of the francophone countries plus a representative from an agricultural institute. There has, nevertheless, been significant continuity among national participants attending subregional meetings which in turn has promoted the development of camaraderie within the organization, enhancing cooperation, sharing, trust, and commitment. Women, while under-represented, have constituted between one-fourth and one-third of the participants who have been engaged in the workshops.

FUNDING

As noted earlier, IDRC has been a major funder of ERNWACA since its inception. Substantial help has also been made available by USAID and support has been received from UNESCO, UNICEF, and Donors to African Education, in addition to the French, Swedish, and Netherlands economic assistance programs. Not being able to depend uniquely on one donor for an assured level of financial support obviously creates problems for ERNWACA and requires constant and intensive fund-raising efforts. On the other hand, this diversity of financial support also means that ERNWACA has greater control over its own programs, projects, and goals and thus avoids becoming a donor surrogate. In a sense, the pattern of funding insures that ERNWACA can continue to represent a Western and Central African perspective in its educational research mission. It also means that ERNWACA has to monitor its expenditures.

THE EDUCATIONAL RESEARCH
NETWORK IN KENYA

Daniel N. Sifuna

The Educational Research Network in Kenya (ERNIKE) is a registered association, whose main purpose is to promote educational research activities in the country. It was founded in September 1988 as an affiliate of the Educational Research Network in Eastern and Southern Africa (ERNESA). Some of ERNIKE's aims and objectives are to identify and execute research in education, disseminate research findings, and build educational research capacity in Kenya.

Membership in the network is open to all academic staff in institutions of higher learning, educational researchers, policy makers, educational administrators, and postgraduate students interested in education issues. Administratively, ERNIKE has an executive committee which consists of a chairman, secretary, treasurer, and committee members. Links with various institutions in the country are made through liaison officers.

At the regional level, ERNIKE participates in the various ERNESA-organized programs. Contacts with ERNESA are made through the chairperson of ERNIKE, who is a trustee of the regional body.

Since its formation, ERNIKE has carried out a number of research activities. Through an IDRC research grant it has accomplished the following:

- collection of annotated bibliographies on recent educational research
- compilation of inventories of available research reports and current research projects
- preparation of state-of-the art reviews of three priority areas in education
- publication of a newsletter
- organization of research training workshops and dissemination seminars

- a book entitled *Issues in Educational Research in Africa*, is currently under production with East African Educational Publishers Ltd.

ERNIKE hosted the ERNESA Regional Planning Meeting in May 1991 and has successfully completed the UNICEF-sponsored research on the "Girl Child" project. ERNIKE has been solely supported by IDRC, except for small funds generated from registration fees. This has made it difficult for the network to hold meetings and carry out its activities on a regular basis. Without alternative sources of funding the network is unlikely to accomplish its aims and objectives.[1]

NOTE

1. For further information contact: ADEN Interim Office, P. O. Box 1483, Machakos, Kenya. Tel: (0145) 30536; Fax: (0145) 21188.

THE BOTSWANA EDUCATIONAL RESEARCH ASSOCIATION'S PARTICIPATION IN RESEARCH AND POLICY STUDIES FOR THE NATIONAL COMMISSION OF EDUCATION

Changu Mannathoko

The Botswana Educational Research Association (BERA) is currently undertaking research and policy studies for the second National Commission on Education (NCE). BERA views this as a major step forward in its goal of developing dialogue and collaboration between educational researchers and policy makers. The involvement of BERA in research and policy studies for NCE is also raising the status of BERA and strengthening the national research capacity.

The Botswana government set up the second NCE in July 1992; the first was fifteen years before in 1977. The 1977 commission conducted an in-depth and wide-ranging review of Botswana's entire education system, its goals and major problems. The commission report formed the basis for the National Policy of Education which was detailed in Government Paper number 1 of 1977. The 1992 commission was set up to review Botswana's education system. It is paying particular attention to the structure and content of secondary education in the context of the country's present and future economic and social change, development, and problems. The commission is addressing a growing perception by education interest groups that educational planning and development needs to be more job oriented and human development based. To be relevant, education should be sensitive and responsive to Botswana's increasingly complex and diverse economy.

As is customary in all government commissions, the government has invited all members of society and interest groups to make oral and/or written submissions to it. The commissioners are traveling throughout the country getting oral submissions from members of the public.

The composition of the 1992 commission shows a dramatic shift from the 1977 commission. In all it has twelve members, only four of whom are foreigners—unlike the 1977 commission which had only two nationals out of six commissioners. The 1977 commissioners were all educators, while only three of the eight nationals are educators and the other five members of the 1992 commission are either from the private sector or from the Ministries of Finance and Development Planning, Commerce, and Industry. This time there are five females, while in 1977 all were men. The four foreign members are from Germany, Malaysia, Singapore, and Britain, with the intention that they should bring information and experience directed at addressing issues related to the link between education and economic development, employment, science, and technology.

BOTSWANA EDUCATIONAL RESEARCH ASSOCIATION (BERA) AND POLICY RESEARCH FOR THE COMMISSION

Once establishment of the NCE had been announced in July 1992, BERA decided to prepare both oral and written submissions for it. BERA invited senior education researchers to prepare research-based papers on critical education issues which made up elements of the BERA position paper to the commission. They covered the following policy issues: (1) educational structure and quality of education, (2) gender and education policy, (3) education, schooling, and language policy, (4) quality of teacher education, (5) community schooling and education policy, and (6) quality of basic education. These papers were presented at a one-day public BERA seminar in 1992. It was well attended and members of the public made rigorous critical comments on all the papers presented. After the seminar, two BERA researchers were charged with editing the papers and preparing the BERA position paper for final submission to the commission.

BERA's Policy Research for the National Commission

Following this seminar, there were discussions between BERA and the commission about its capacity to undertake research and policy studies for the commission. It was a fulfilling event for BERA when the commission secretariat formally appointed BERA as its agent for undertaking a number of research and policy studies on education. BERA was requested to work on the following issues:

1. policy options for preschool education
2. policy options for vocationalization of senior secondary education
3. quality of primary school completers and the implications for Form 1 organization and teaching
4. policy options for transition rates from junior secondary to senior secondary education
5. strategies for the improvement of math and science performance at all levels of the education system
6. policy options for the development and administration of tertiary education
7. policy options for education research
8. evaluation of technician and artisan training in Botswana

9. update of learning opportunities in Botswana and survey of private English-medium primary schools

BERA was delighted to accept the challenging offer and immediately selected researchers to develop proposals, according to their expertise in the subject matter. Some researchers selected were not BERA members but were approached because they are the best in the field. Studies are to be completed by the end of January.

Capacity-Building and Consultancy Fees

This major consultancy for BERA is definitely an important step in strengthening research capacity-building in Botswana. BERA as a national research network has been given the opportunity to coordinate and undertake policy research for the NCE, and high-quality research will impact on our future national education policy. BERA is paid by the NCE for this consultancy and in that way is contributing to the organization's financial sustainability. In turn, BERA has since 1991 had a consultancy policy which states that out of each consultant's fees it retains ten percent; it has so far earned a modest income through putting that policy into practice.

NETWORKING IN SOUTH AFRICA: AN AID TO INSTITUTIONAL DEVELOPMENT

David Gilmour

Until recently South African educators have for political reasons not been able to network formally with colleagues in the subregion except on either a sporadic or a personal level. Internally, the organization of education interest groups reflected the apartheid divisions so that similarly there has been little contact between different education institutions and societies.

Now, with moves on the political front there are more avenues for communication opening up. One instance has been the development of Education Policy Units at several universities (Witwatersrand, Durban-Westville, Western Cape, and more recently Fort Hare). These have in common prodemocratic positions which facilitate interaction.

A second example in this vein has been the 1993 National Education Policy Investigation which has brought together nearly 400 researchers. A third broader-based example has been the formation in 1991 of a professional society, the Southern African Comparative and History of Education Society (SACHES), which has the express purpose of linking South African with Southern African educators. The admission of SACHES to the World Council of Comparative Education Societies in 1992 has provided an acceptable forum for the meeting of educators and hopefully this forum will expand.

The first major conference was held in South Africa in October 1992, and attracted participants from Zambia, Botswana, Mozambique, Zimbabwe, and Namibia. The enthusiasm for this modest venture expressed by colleagues to the north of South Africa was salutary and illustrated quite unequivocally the need for further and systematic contact. The concerns that were raised by delegates reflected some of the broader difficulties around networking in South Africa. A key issue for delegates was how to sustain contacts and how to link with existing networks (for example ERNESA, BERA, BOLESWA, etc.) in a complementary way. While all agreed in principle that such networks were invaluable, the main obstacles were seen on the one hand to be financial and technical and on the other to do with scope of interest.

In respect of finances, South African academics have limited university resources to call on, in general being restricted to one conference-type trip per annum. For many others, particularly those at so-called "black" universities and at teachers' colleges, there are no sources of funding. This clearly limits the opportunities for direct interaction. Similarly, there are limited computer network possibilities. This seems to apply equally for colleagues outside South Africa.

In terms of scope of interest, there remains in South Africa a division of concerns between those primarily involved in initial teacher training and the more academic concerns of university-based educators. Again there are historical reasons for this related to issues of access to schools, political attitudes, and perceived status differentials. Hopefully, this may change as the shape of the tertiary education structure is replanned, but at the moment conferences and meetings are both physically separate and tend to deal with different foci. Similarly there are jurisdictional difficulties and political hostilities that need to be overcome.

Given these constraints, it became clear that if face-to-face contact was to take place, conferences and meetings would have to be coordinated (e.g., piggybacking) and that funding was crucial. In this respect up-to-date mailing lists and information exchanges were seen to be important. In general, knowledge about different areas of research is at a premium. More information about existing networks and research activities is essential for developing networks.

The mechanisms to do this are of course another set of issues and relate to a second dimension, namely the development of existing strengths and initiatives in a way that does not permit control over research activity and dissemination and that is enabling rather than, as has tended to be the case, exclusive. The initiatives referred to above are expressly concerned with this principle and indeed the long-term success of any networking efforts will rest on democratizing and equalizing research efforts and institutions. In this sense, the principle of networking has great potential for assisting in the opening up of educational activity to the fullest range of stakeholders.

NETWORKING IN SUPPORT OF SOUTH AFRICAN POLICY CHANGE

Peter Badcock-Walters

The Education Foundation is an independent, nongovernment, nonprofit and politically nonaligned development institute committed to the creation of a new and appropriate education system for South Africa. Thus the foundation is centrally located in a networking and facilitation process to ensure genuine consultation and cooperative relationships around policy development and system design. This entails interactive and open working relationships across the stakeholder spectrum, including the incumbent bureaucracy and technocracy.

By definition, this separates the networking process on to at least two levels. The first, reflecting the popular notion of contact points within a field of interest, is a continuing process of information sharing and the creation of access to data. The foundation has established an education data and information clearing house, EduSource, to facilitate this process. EduSource maintains an extensive network of data sources and NGO contacts to ensure equalization of access to historically restricted data, and to inform both the dialogue process and the range of key role players within it. This level of networking also involves developing relationships with other contact networks within South Africa, and a listing of these. Beyond the country's borders, relationships are being established with ERNESA/BERA, as well as with policy and data analysts in several neighboring states including Botswana, Zimbabwe, Swaziland, and Namibia.

At a second and essentially strategic level, the networking process involves those role players directly engaged in the formulation, articulation, and development of policy and education futures in regard to basic and postsecondary education, governance, teacher supply, and financing. It is here that the Education Foundation is involved in a number of process focal points:

1. The development of resources and technologies, including computer-based policy modeling tools, to empower South Africans to formulate and advance policy options and positions.

2. The facilitation of forums and environments in which this policy dialogue process can be advanced in a climate of cooperation and consensus seeking.

3. The creation of policy support systems, including a highly mobile support unit, to ensure the transfer of skills and technologies to the widest range of South African role players (and their support networks).

4. The input of comparative international information and innovative alternatives to stimulate debate and the interrogation of policy positions.

This second level of activity involves a comparatively limited number of South Africans, reflecting the critical shortage of skilled or experienced human resources in the policy field. As a consequence, the foundation's areas of focus have the cumulative effect of orienting and training stakeholder and interest groups, and expanding those human resources needed to address the education crisis. The Education Foundation is supported in these activities by its institutional links with the Research Triangle Institute (RTI) of North Carolina, which provide both advanced policy modeling technologies and comparative international experience.

Although unrelated to some extent to these policy support systems and networks, the foundation is also involved in the research, development, and piloting of an appropriate community college system for South Africa. As a result an extremely extensive network of role players and interest groups in adult basic, postsecondary, and bridging education has been established to concentrate energy on the piloting and establishment of a college system.[1]

NOTE

1. The Education Foundation and EduSource may be contacted at: Johannesburg, Tel: 011:886 7874, Fax: 011:886 8069 or Durban, Tel: 031:305 2401, Fax: 031:305 5571.

EDUCATIONAL NETWORKING IN FRENCH-SPEAKING WEST AFRICA: HOPE OR FALLACY?

Michel Carton

In their analysis, *The Status of Educational Research and Policy Analysis in Sub-Saharan Africa*, Namuddu and Tapsoba (1993) list more than thirty references on the topic. Only two relate to French-speaking Africa (more precisely, Burkina-Faso).[1]

In his chapter devoted to West and Central Africa, Tapsoba points out some of the specific characteristics of the French-speaking countries in terms of educational research:

- training in educational research as a distinct area of specialization is lacking
- very few universities have faculties of education
- training in education, based on the French model, is provided in teacher training colleges and focuses essentially on classroom approaches
- further training in educational action-oriented research for teachers is not conceived as a means of promotion and/or problem solving, as promotion is based on years of service.

As far as the universities are concerned, Tapsoba pinpoints the following problems: (1) faculty members are part of the civil service: their promotion does not depend on their current research activities, unless it is related to a Doctorat d'Etat which is in itself a promotion instrument; (2) faculty members have heavy teaching duties; (3) only a few postgraduate programs are based in the universities and the few existing ones are in the *ecoles normales supérieures* which are geared toward training teachers and not researchers; and (4) infrastructures (libraries, documentation centers, computers) are in very bad shape (The National Centre for Education in Cameroon has not subscribed to a research journal since its creation as a research institution in 1973); most educational research facilities are in a total state of chaos.

The combination of the general situation in the universities and of the poor status of educational research explains why it is surprising to attend a meeting like the symposium held in July 1992 at the National University of Lesotho, under the auspices of the Botswana, Lesotho, and Swaziland Educational Research Association (BOLESWA), where more than one hundred participants gathered for five days to discuss the relations between theory and practice in educational research. Such an event cannot (yet?) be envisaged in the French-speaking African countries. Furthermore, as pointed out for Botswana, "current research . . . is not influencing educational change and development as much as it could 'but even if' research appears to have assumed for itself a reactive rather than a proactive role" (Nyati-Ramahobo and Prophet, n.d., p. 37). Even so, it is much better than what has been noted by Tapsoba in Burkina-Faso where "a policy analyst at Ouagadougou University indicated that the authorities tend to implement policy that has been rejected by researchers. Officials appear to be uninformed about existing analyses, or they choose to ignore them" (Namuddu and Tapsoba, 1993, p. 51). How to explain these differences and how to relate them to our concern for networking?

THE AFRICAN STATES: STRUCTURES OR FACTIONS?

The debate concerning the nature of the African states is the main element to be considered in answering the previous question. Referring to the work of Bayart (1989), it can be assumed that the African states, especially in French-speaking Africa, and the so-called "civil society" are not two separate elements in a country. They are intrinsically connected in all kinds of networks controlled by some sociopolitical factions, built on some ever-moving combinations of parenthood, ethnicity, religion, and residence. The "big men" gain their power, in the state and the society, by making ad hoc syntheses of these elements. In that sense the conflicts between factions are a mode of production of the political life and not a disintegration factor of the society, as these factions control both the state system and the numerous networks composing the society. "The post colonial state lives like a rhizome and not like a roots system. It is composed of a multifaceted multiplicity of networks, the underground stalks of which connect some scattered points of the society" (Bayart, 1989, p. 272).

The networks controlled by the factions are then, in French-speaking Africa more than elsewhere, the key component of the social and the economic functioning: the conflicts between factions are not only about the power and status of their fluctuant members. These conflicts concern also the appropriation of wealth in a context of material scarceness and political instability. As a consequence, some short-term considerations are often more valuable, as far as action is concerned, than long-term planning.

The more rigid and centralized nature of the French-speaking postcolonial African states, in comparison with that of the English-speaking ones, might explain the greater visibility of the influence of factions and networks in the concerned countries. In the Anglo-Saxon inspired societies, the separation between the state structure, the local authorities, and the pressure groups of all kinds is less strong and gives some kind of legitimacy to different social organizations which can more easily combine the factional and professional dimensions.

The Relative Autonomy of Education and the State

In the education field, professional networks and associations are much more influential in the English-speaking countries than in the French-speaking ones, as they combine some modern and traditional elements. Educationists in French-speaking Africa are mostly members of trade unions which are more concerned, as factions, with political games aimed at controlling the state than with professional and education problems. This occurs because the state is, formally at least, a relatively autonomous body.

The education field is then a good illustration of the above-mentioned analysis concerning the nature of the state. As pinpointed by Hallak and Tobelem (1993), "the education sector serves as a means to preserve some vested interests and to gain some dominating positions—or, more precisely, to facilitate the gaining of some more or less confessable personal interest—it then scarcely possesses an internal institutional capacity corresponding with the ambitions of its officially proclaimed objectives."

This analysis of the internal functioning of any educational system (not only in Africa, as it appears from the Hallak and Tobelem statement) fits very well with Bayart's description of the rhizome state. But the analysis does not correspond fully to it, as the authors consider the institutional environment of the education system:

> The educational policies have too long been defined according to some illegitimate decision-making process. This may have happened because the decision-makers themselves could not be considered as legitimate or because the populations did not feel concerned by the set up priorities.... The disclosure of some forbidden but not repressed actions ... ends up in the feeling that there is not much to expect from societies unable to sanction the irresponsibility of corruption or the decision-makers. Everything is permitted, as the local "cultures" are considered as a fatality.... The more the gap enlarges itself between the leaders and populations, the more the education sector is vulnerable and inefficient. Every statement aiming at doing more in education without a strong parallel development of the institutional capacity leads to a fantastic wastage of resources. (Hallak & Tobelem, 1993, p. 3)

In principle, we can't but accept this position! But, as usual, the reality is somewhere in between this obvious statement and the recognition of the heavy influence of the local cultures mentioned above.

EDUCATIONAL NETWORKS: A PART OF THE FACTION SYSTEM?

The question of networking in the field of educational research in French-speaking West Africa can only be seen in that framework. Is it possible, in that respect, to launch some educational research which goes beyond the limits of school curriculum and pedagogy, which has an influence (even limited) on decision makers and aims at developing some professionalism in that field? A Senegalese situation can give some hints in that respect.

The Association for the Development of Education and Training in Africa (ADEF) was launched in 1992 in Senegal (despite its continental title!) following a constituent assembly of more than 200 people composed of a majority of teachers, plus education managers, project leaders, and all the researchers of the National Institute for the Development of Education (INEADE). The executive secretary was then appointed as minister for literacy!

Two interpretations can then be made: either the association is the first step of a professionalization movement in the field of education and training action-oriented research, or it is a faction-oriented structure. The two interpretations are correct at the same time if we follow our initial analysis of the French-speaking African society. (Even though Senegal is a specific case because of its "democratic" nature.)

It is interesting to underline that the newly established structure has defined itself as an association and not as a network. This consideration leads to the question posed in the title of this document: is it conceptually and functionally appropriate to speak of networks in the sociopolitical context described concerning French-speaking Africa (and perhaps in other parts of the continent)? Is it not misleading to use a term which in fact reflects a social function which might be considered as one of the causes of the crises (economic and education) in which Africa is today? Would it not be better to speak of structures and/or systems which refer to some universes with boundaries and possibly a center? Networking is useful in the contexts where professional and/or academic structures represent a blockage for communication and innovation (some networks tend too easily to become structured by leaving apart the characteristics of any network: nonhierarchical organization, no center, and the principle of aperture). In that respect, the situation of ERNESA seems to indicate that a balance can be found between a networked traditional society and a structured modern society. Is this possible in French-speaking Africa? The new Educational Research Network for Western and Central Africa (ERNWACA) will give us the answer in a few years time.

NOTE

1. A search for educational research in French-speaking Africa at the IBE-Geneva and UNESCO-Paris libraries turned up only four more documents.

ASIA

PART V

We do not have a lot of information on networks in Asia. India is totally absent in this collection, and we catch only glimpses of the enormous activity in educational research in China. One explanation may be our cultural ignorance as implied in the paper by Cheng. The traditional emphasis on North-South communication has meant we talked, they listened, and so we haven't learned much.

In fact there is a long tradition of educational research in Asia. Because this developed largely independent of recent pressures for uniformization in the social sciences, the research no doubt differs in some fundamental ways from that which we do. Perhaps we would not be comfortable with all that Chinese and Indian researchers offer as examples of high-quality scientific work.

Furthermore, Cheng suggests, in China at least, boundaries of networks are sharply drawn, and it is not likely that it will be possible to develop an open system network of the kind championed, for example, by King. This would appear to limit the effectiveness of networking as a process of mutual production of information and knowledge.

At the same time, however, there is evidence of the development of networks that link policy makers and researchers. [Ed. note: Cheng is too modest to note that he has carried out several important studies on research and policy making in China.] Seen from the outside, these networks in China seem similar in structure to those found in Africa and Latin America and the North, that is Europe and the United States.

Does the presence and activity of these networks contradict the assertions of Cheng? If so, how can we resolve those contradictions?

APPRECIATING CULTURES: EDUCATIONAL RESEARCH AND NETWORKING IN EAST ASIA

Cheng Kai-ming

Networking in educational research has been happening in many parts of the world. Although it is not always without difficulties, and successes in some of the regions are yet to materialize, the communication and interaction generated from even the attempts to establish networks are remarkable. Many of these networks have achieved what international organizations should have done but failed to do, and certainly have gone beyond what governments could achieve.

On the other hand, the kind of networking which is happening elsewhere does not seem to appeal to communities in East Asia. Although the East Asian never rejected any opinion about networking in educational research, and indeed some primitive form of networking is likely to emerge in the near future, an examination of the culture of these communities in the context of educational research and networking reveals some differences from other regions.

It has to be mentioned at the beginning that the study of culture is a lifelong career. What is expressed here are my observations based on my experience in the field and my understanding of other cultures. Many of the observations are inspired by related studies in psychology, philosophy, and management studies. However, comprehensive theories about the East Asian culture have yet to emerge. The points expressed in this paper are hypotheses awaiting confirmation.

A CULTURE ISOLATED

The East Asian societies are Japan, Korea, Hong Kong, Taiwan, and mainland China, with the possible inclusion of Vietnam. These societies share the use of chopsticks and the use of Chinese characters as part or whole of their written language. They were all once influenced by Confucius and Mencius, and are often referred to as the Confucian societies. How the thinking of Confucius and Mencius actually affected these societies, and how they are responsible for societies three

thousand years after their death are basically questions unanswered. At best, responses to these questions are done by East Asian scholars in frameworks not always
appreciated by scholars elsewhere, and most of them are in the local languages.

There have always been efforts in the West to understand the culture in East
Asian societies, but there are factors that have made such efforts difficult. The
difficulty in the languages is one. That these societies have never been completely
colonized by a Western power, with the exception of Hong Kong,[1] could be another.
However, the most prohibiting factor is the inward-looking characteristic of the
culture.

Ironically, one of the conclusions on which all studies about the East Asian
culture converge is that it places high value on social relations (Adler, 1986; Bond,
1991). However, social relations in East Asian societies are hinged upon a formal
structure, often a hierarchy, which is taken for granted. Relations outside this given
structure is often seen as irrelevant, if not odd. Hence, interaction within the society
is intensive, but interactions outside the society are taken with caution. This has
made the societies in East Asia often seem indifferent, sometimes even hostile, to
external efforts to understand their culture. In a world which is rapidly moving
toward integration, the isolation of the East Asian culture from the rest of the world
has put the culture into a rather uneasy position.

The study of culture is always difficult. Either you know too much of it so that
you take a lot for granted, or you know too little of it to claim any understanding.
The closed nature of the East Asian culture has made studies of it even more
difficult. Hence, the culture in East Asian communities remains rather unknown
and often distorted.

A Society Structured

The structured nature of East Asian societies has affected networking in the region.
Earlier studies of East Asian culture often emphasize the importance of family in the
culture. This notion should also be applied to social relations at large. Fei (1981), in
his seminal work begun a half century ago, describes the Chinese society as a series of
ripples, with people's attention concentrated on the inner circles. Affairs in the outer
circles are often not on the agenda. He refers to this pattern of social relations as a
"configuration of hierarchy" in which every member has a place in the hierarchy. Each
member is very conscious of his or her own position in the hierarchy, and will act
accordingly. Fei contrasts this with what he calls the "configuration of association"
which is prevalent in Western societies. In the West, individuals interact with one
another as equals and become associated because of necessity. There are still hierarchies, but first, there is not only one consistent pattern of hierarchy; second, the
hierarchies are ad hoc in nature, with no preset social codes attached to them. Although
Fei's work is mainly on Chinese societies, it can easily be borrowed with comparative
ease to analyze other East Asian societies.

Fei's framework may help explain many of the features identified as characteristics of education in East Asia. It helps explain, for example, the general tendency
of conformity and uniformity in the education systems. Students are expected to

follow more or less the same curriculum and sit the same examination, hence the severe competition. Students are required to follow the same codes of behavior, hence the strict training for discipline (Bond, 1991, pp. 11–14). It helps explain, as another example, the emphasis on moral aspects of education as superior to knowledge and skills, because social relations are the most essential element for survival in society. The importance of social relations as compared with performance is identified by many observers of East Asian organizations (e.g., Redding, 1990; Ronen, 1986, pp. 146–47).

IMPLICATIONS FOR NETWORKING

Following Fei's metaphor, people in East Asian societies tend to pay most attention to the innermost circles, and become less and less interested in affairs in the outer circles.

The implications for networking are therefore understandable. As mentioned elsewhere (Cheng, 1991), networking in East Asia is most likely through formal or official channels.[2] Even when there are no legal or political barriers, relations within the established framework are seen as more comfortable and secure. However, networking is effective only when it works across institutions and organizations, that is, outside the established framework. This is rather foreign to East Asian societies.

In mainland China, the situation is exacerbated by the complex formal organization of the society under ideologies of planned economy.[3] Even now when the formal organizations are collapsing, when people or organizations interact, matching (*duikou*) is important. In brief, only persons or organizations of comparable states are seen as acceptable counterparts. This is not based on necessity, nor is it based on any kind of cost-benefit calculations. It is a kind of protocol deeply rooted in the culture. It is a kind of code which is not in the book but on people's minds. Networking even within the country is not without difficulties. Often, the competition for leadership (in other words, definition of a new hierarchy which is not granted) overtakes considerations of mutual benefits. With the downfall of the planned economy, people are struggling with traditional bindings and learning to interact with one another on totally new bases.

However, there is a strong consensus among scholars in East Asian communities that international networking is important, although they are less ready to participate in constructing networks than to enjoy the benefits of networking. The general favor for networking is there, except that the way to effective networking is blocked by unfavorable traditions among the community.

There are dynamics which may eventually lead to effective networking. Taiwan, for example, has recently established a research foundation which tries to pool together researchers in Taiwan, mainland China, and Hong Kong. The foundation, as is demonstrated by its first symposium,[4] carries a strong emphasis on education. The comparative education societies in the East Asian countries have also had considerable opportunities to interact with one another. That might well become a basis for networking within East Asia. It is a slow yet effective process. It takes time to break away from a culture that has been with the people for thousands of years.

International Network Helps

Given the inward-looking culture, it is understandable that networks in a larger international community may not be readily helpful to facilitate networking within East Asia. However, sincerity from larger international networks may still play a positive role. The following are some observations.

First, the cultural isolation as mentioned earlier has also led to a lack of understanding of the culture of educational research in East Asia. The natural scientists from East Asian scholars are readily accepted by the international community, many of them are extremely active and highly regarded in their respective disciplines. This happens only occasionally in the realm of social sciences, and education in particular. One explanation for this is that natural sciences are less concerned with social relations and hence scholars in East Asia find little difficulty in communicating with scholars elsewhere. Social sciences intensively involve social relations and hence entertain diverse philosophies and methodology about research. This is certainly visible in education. There are huge bodies of literature which is generated by research within respective East Asian communities. In China alone, a recent survey reckoned that there are over 6,500 full-time educational researchers in higher education or research institutes, and around 120,000 full-time educational researchers at all levels of local departments. They produce enormous amounts of research output. However, little of this is known to people outside China, partly because they are only available in Chinese, partly because the methodology is not seen as acceptable by international standards.[5] The same is also true in Japan, Korea, and Taiwan. All the research activity and product affects teaching and learning in schools, but little is known to the external world. An effort to understand and appreciate the research paradigms and outputs in East Asia could be the first way that international networks find a part to play.

Second, the writer has argued elsewhere against the North-South or donor-recipient paradigm which is prevalent in the international scene (Cheng, 1991). Often international interactions in educational research have virtually degenerated into a donor-recipient dialogue. NORRAG could be an exception where there are also North-North interactions, although its concern is still business in the South. There is very little South-South interaction, although the RRAGs are starting to carry this dimension. North learning from South is simply inconceivable.

The difficulty with this North-South paradigm in the context of East Asia is that many of the countries in the region are nowhere in the North-South map. Apart from China which is admittedly in the South, and perhaps apart from Japan which is beginning to become active in playing a donor role, the other communities are neither donors nor recipients. It is therefore often difficult for them to enter international conversations which usually take place within the North-South dimension. The education systems and practices in all the East Asian communities are very similar. The approaches to educational research are again similar. The North-South division in the realm of educational research is artificial.

Although it is understandable that most research activities are donor driven, it is perhaps exactly the mission of networks such as NORRAG to move away from the donor-recipient paradigm and identify alternative frameworks that would better serve educational purposes. The East Asian communities may provide the litmus test of the success of international networks in achieving this mission.

NOTES

1. Korea, Taiwan, and a large part of China were all once colonized by Japan. There were "concessions" in China which were virtual colonies of Western powers, but they were only small pieces of land colonized for a short while.

2. This is also attributable to another factor which will not be elaborated here: Authority in East Asian societies often originates from officialdom. See Pye (1985) for detailed discussions.

3. One may also turn this around and argue that it was because of the tradition of the planned society that countries have been able to survive for so long.

4. Held in Taipei in August 1993 with the participation of 26 social scientists from mainland China.

5. See details in Cheng (1991).

SOUTH EAST ASIA BIBLIOGRAPHIC AND ABSTRACTING SERVICE

Zainal Ghani

In the course of carrying out its activities, the South East Asia Research Review and Advisory Group (SEARRAG) identified several problems associated with educational research in the region. One of the main problems is the accessibility and the dissemination of the vast amount of research found in countries which make up SEARRAG. For example, the Philippines has identified more than 7,000 researches, Thailand about 5,000, Indonesia about 3,500, and Malaysia about 1,200 researches. However, most of this high volume of educational research is not accessible to all concerned with education, either at the country level or at the regional level. The main reasons for this inaccessibility are (1) the bulk (about 85 percent) of the research are theses and dissertations, and (2) most of the rest of the research is commissioned, which usually means that this research is confidential.

In the Southeast Asian region another major problem is the language used in the research in the different countries which means that most research in countries such as Indonesia, Thailand, and Malaysia is not accessible to persons in other countries.

Given problems of low access to educational research, how can SEARRAG organize a network that permits achievement of its objective of enhancing the contribution of educational research to the improvement of educational policy, research, and practices in the region? The response has been the establishment of the South East Asia Bibliographic and Abstracting Service (SEABAS). Through this service, information on the numerous researches available is collected and disseminated to people at all levels of education in the region in the form of abstracts prepared in English.

SEABAS carries out two major activities at both the national and the regional levels: (1) identification, collection, storage, and dissemination of abstracts of local research and (2) publication and dissemination of bibliographies, thematic collections of abstracts and state-of-the-art reviews. In recent years, SEABAS has become SEARRAG's major activity.

To improve its functionality and sustainability, SEABAS now consists of a regional center in each SEARRAG country. The regional center is sited at the Unit of Research in Basic Education, University of Science, Malaysia. The national centers are situated in institutions which have close access to research information on the one hand and, on the other, have linkages for dissemination with the different groups of potential users of the information. In Malaysia, Thailand, Indonesia, and Philippines the national collection centers for SEABAS are units or divisions in ministries of education. The Indonesian SEABAS national collection center is with the Office of Educational and Cultural Research and Development (Balitbang Dikbud). The Malaysian center is at the Educational Planning and Research Division and the Philippine center at the National Educational Testing and Research Centre. In the case of Thailand, the SEABAS national center is at the National Education Commission which is under Thailand's Prime Minister's office. In Singapore and Brunei, the national centers are at the university libraries of the National Institute of Education of the Nanyang Technological University and the University of Brunei Durassalam, respectively.

As a result of the development of the SEABAS database, each national center has now two databases on educational research information. The first database is based on the contributions from all the national centers. This regional database of educational research information is in English so as to ensure international dissemination. The other is a national database prepared in the official language of the country to provide access to local users. With these two databases the access to educational research is thus widened.

The regional SEABAS database uses CDS-ISIS software and now consists of 4,200 bibliographic records and 1,500 abstracts. These records are accessible through the use of keywords or descriptors based on the UNESCO-IBE thesaurus. The regional center and the national collection centers can retrieve and forward any requests for information on the basis of the keywords or descriptors sent from people both within and outside the region.

SEABAS is now in the process of distributing its database worldwide on a subscription basis. It is proposed that for an annual subscription of U.S.$100, subscribers will be provided with the regional collection and an update every six months (to be forwarded on diskettes) and all SEARRAG publications. These publications will consist of state-of-the-art review reports, bibliographies, thematic compilations, of abstracts and books on regional synthesis of reviews on specific topics.[1]

NOTE

1. Those interested in subscribing to the SEABAS database can contact Zainal Ghani, SEABAS, Unit for Research in Basic Education, UPPA, University Sains Malaysia, 11800 Penang, Malaysia. Names and addresses of contact persons at the other centers are in Appendix 1.

EUROPE

PART VI

Networks pursue different objectives and different strategies, in response partly to the context in which they are operating, but also as a function of their stage of development. Watson suggests three levels of development: professional, institutional, and political. Note the parallels to the works in Part I by Carton, King, and Lauglo. Watson offers several examples of how researchers have banded together to share data and ideas. Sometimes these associations have focused on applications, rather than on research proper. In this case researchers join up with managers and educators. The major constraint to this kind of activity is the growing difficulty of finding finance.

Some associations have turned to universities (and some universities have invited in or have formed associations) as a method to fund activities. The universities benefit from increased visibility and sometimes from fees earned for contract work. At this level there is perhaps more opportunity to influence policy.

It is at the third level that researchers can reach beyond academic confines to associate with the likes of government and donor agency officials and non-governmental organizations. Watson offers the fairly new Oxford Conference (second meeting held in 1993, next in 1995) as a successful example of a network that crosses lines.

Contrast that effort with the more professional associations described in the brief contributions by Richmond, Entwistle, and Karcher. In each case one can see how an association of friends and colleagues has matured into a more substantial, and formal, organization complete with newsletter and has begun to consider reaching beyond their borders to contact policy makers directly.

Properly speaking, the German Foundation for International Development (DSE) is not a network, but rather is a network generator or network inducer. But here too one can see a process of evolution of activities. Gmelin describes how programmatic activities have expanded from sponsorship of individual researchers and educators to identification of institutions that take on responsibilities for network maintenance and growth. A major problem here is that of sustainability. Many of the institutions can survive only if linked with and supported by others with a better financial base.

Not all North-based networks seek to influence the South. The contribution by Gray is included to show how networks can be organized for the purpose of changing their membership. The Scottish Education Action for Development (SEAD) effort deserves special attention.

PROFESSIONAL ASSOCIATIONS AND ACADEMIC NETWORKS: SOME OBSERVATIONS FOR THE UNITED KINGDOM

Keith Watson

Very few academics or researchers in international education in the United Kingdom operate from large professional bases. They might be in large institutional departments (e.g., university faculties or departments of education [UDES]) but they might be the only person with a specific research interest in comparative/international education. This has largely resulted from financial stringency and staff reductions over the past fifteen years or so. At the most there will be a handful of colleagues with similar research or teaching interests. An exception to this is the unique Department of Comparative and International Education at the University of London Institute of Education.

How academics and researchers keep abreast of developments and how they can exert any influence, professional or political, are issues of considerable concern. Personal and professional contacts and networks are, therefore, of great importance. This short chapter will explore three levels of networking: (1) personal/academic links through professional associations, (2) institutional developments, and (3) moves toward political pressure groups (see Figure 3).

LEVEL 1: ACADEMIC NETWORKING

At the most basic first level there has always been interaction between friends and colleagues in the same or in different institutions but the most important pattern of academic networking is through professional societies and academic journals where research and ideas are openly discussed.

The British Comparative and International Education Society (BCIES), founded in 1965, with a fairly constant membership of 150–160, is an obvious example. Its members have both European and Third World interests and several of them are also members of the French Comparative Education Society (AFEC) or the North American Comparative and International Education Society (CIES), and attend the World

Figure 3
Levels of Networking

Level 1: Academic Networking

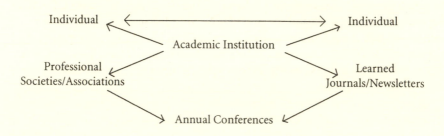

Level 2: Institutional Networking/Consortia

Level 3: Networking for Political Pressure

Congress of Comparative Education Societies, all of which hold international meetings at regular intervals. The society keeps its membership informed of activities, regional/day conferences and so forth through a newsletter. The BCIES journal, *Compare*, in its thirteenth volume, is now published three times a year. Although, only a few papers now come from society members it keeps colleagues informed of developments elsewhere. Recent annual conferences (held in September) have sought to bring together academics from different disciplines such as law, assessment, science, and politics. Conference proceedings usually appear in book form.

The considerably smaller British Association of Teachers and Researchers in Overseas Education (BATROE) is essentially oriented toward the Third World.

When originally founded in the 1960s, its common link was to bring together academics and administrators with a pastoral concern for overseas students. As a result, of all the professional societies, it had close links with government through the British Council and the Overseas Development Administration (ODA), representatives of whom sit on the executive committee. However, as this society has moved toward more academic conferences, the links with ODA have been weakened and the capacity of BATROE to influence policy, rather than be told about it, has been undermined. The same can be said of the International Committee of UCET (Universities Council for the Education of Teachers). Their weakness as pressure groups has highlighted the need for a more collaborative network of institutions.

Other professional associations and academic networks which spread far wider than education include the Development Studies Association (DSA) with its separate, but interesting, specialist study groups. Information is imparted through a quarterly newsletter, an annual conference in September, and regional meetings, often with larger societies such as the British Educational Research Association (BERA) and the British Educational Management and Administration Society (BEMAS). Such joint meetings have brought together scholars who, under normal circumstances, would not have come into contact with each other. There are also numerous geographically focused groups and specialist associations. Among the former would be the African Studies Association of the United Kingdom (ASAUK), the Association of Southeast Asian Studies in the United Kingdom (ASEASUK), and the Latin American Studies Association (LASA). Specialist groups include science education, English Language Teaching European Education teachers, and so on. Other professional associations are functionally orientated but include an education interest, such as BEMAS, the British Association for Literacy in Development (BALID) and the Commonwealth Association for the Education and Training of Adults (CAETA).

In addition to professional associations are a wide range of nongovernmental organizations (NGOs) such as OXFAM, Christian Aid, and Save the Children Fund which have an educational role in Britain and are concerned with disaster relief and development aid.

Apart from the unique role of *NORRAG News* in keeping an originally select group in touch with current thinking, ongoing research, and forthcoming conferences, two journals need to be mentioned. The *Journal of International Education* seeks to discuss practical issues relating to the pastoral care and recruitment of overseas students studying in Britain. The *International Journal of Educational Development* is specifically oriented toward policy makers, practitioners, and researchers in later developing countries (LDCs).

However valuable these academic societies, journals, and newsletters may be in keeping academics in touch, they do not provide a power base from which government policies can be challenged, or at least critiqued. Nor do they provide a viable means for putting in for collaborative bids for overseas contracts or for attracting large-scale funding. These are beginning to come from the second level of professional networks: institutional centers.

LEVEL 2: INSTITUTIONAL NETWORKING/CONSORTIA

During the past decade there has been a proliferation of international education centers or overseas education units that have been established within faculties and departments of education. Some of these are small; some have brought together colleagues from diverse disciplines such as economics, politics, planning, science, and sociology who share a common interest in international education. Most of these centers are oriented toward LDCs. Others, which subsume education within a wider remit, may be geographically focused, such as, on Africa, Europe, the Middle East or South East Asia.

At the moment most of these centers operate independently and are frequently in competition with one another, especially over courses and bids for contracts. Although academics from within them will know of other colleagues, contacts and networking tend to be on an individual basis. Moves are afoot, however, for closer collaboration between centers and units on a regional basis.

A model already exists on a large scale with the Universities of the North of England Consortium for International Activities (UNECIA). This is a consortium of nine universities with a secretariat based in Sheffield to coordinate overseas contracts using the strengths of the different universities. Discussions are taking place between groups of UDES to see if similar consortia might be developed on a regional basis. The main advantages of this approach would be (1) to draw upon the strengths and expertise of different institutions, (2) to strengthen the power of smaller UDES, and (3) to put in collaborative research bids or run joint courses. The disadvantages, in an age of increased competition, are that some institutional autonomy and sovereignty has to be surrendered and that there has to be an initial financial outlay in order to establish a secretariat. However, the potential for political intervention from a position of strength, if not considerable, is at least enhanced.

LEVEL 3: NETWORKING FOR POLITICAL PRESSURE

The third level of networking is the recent process toward creating a forum of divergent interest groups which would also form a political pressure group. Such was the concern about the fragmentation and diminution of influence of British academics concerned with, or involved in, international/comparative education together with an awareness that academic societies and professional associations and journals in and of themselves are insufficient to mobilize individuals or groups into undertaking practical action or into exerting pressure on policy makers, that a group of academics, representatives of NGOs and agencies such as the Commonwealth Secretariat and the British Council held a series of meetings in 1990. The upshot was the decision to move toward a forum whereby different interest groups could periodically come together to share ideas, learn from each other, and critique policies, all in an atmosphere of mutual collaboration.

The first practical outworking of this group was the organization of the 1991 Oxford Conference which brought together NGOs, bilateral and multilateral aid donors, several ministers of education, academics, and three professional/academic societies: BCIES, BATROE, DSA. In 1991 formal decisions were taken to

1. create a United Kingdom Forum on International Education and Training (UKFIET),
2. hold another Oxford Conference in September 1993,
3. establish a register of ongoing research and researchers,
4. hold periodic meetings, and, when necessary,
5. put forward collective position papers to governments, believing that if these represented the views of several different constituencies, they would have a greater impact than if a series of individual papers appeared in professional journals.

That the process of creating the UKFIET took so long is indicative of the problems arising from trying to systematize collaborative networks. Groups, societies, or organizations need to surrender some of their positions in favor of a greater good. Because of individual mobility the situation is always fluid. Several critical questions have to be answered: Who represents the constituency concerned? Which organizations should be represented? Will certain interest groups cancel out others? Should there be a secretariat for speedy action? Many of these issues remain unresolved. Until there is a sense of vision and general recognition that collaboration is more important than isolation, individuals and institutions will continue to be marginalized or ignored.

SEMINAR ON LATIN AMERICAN EDUCATION, UNITED KINGDOM

Mark Richmond

Following a preliminary meeting at the University of Reading in 1988, a small but gradually increasing group of British-based educationalists and postgraduate students have sustained their interest in Latin American education through a series of one-day conferences in Hull (1989), Bristol (1990), London (1991), and again Hull (1992) and Bristol (1993). As has quickly become customary, the Seminar on Latin American Education, as the group has come to be known, provides not only a forum for established academics and researchers to give papers but also an opportunity for postgraduate students to give short accounts of their research-in-progress or of some topic of interest, in a supportive and encouraging atmosphere. Publications have also developed out of the seminar's activities: papers have subsequently been published in such journals as *Compare* and the *International Journal of Educational Development.*

One offshoot of the seminar was the organization of the first symposium on Latin American education to be held within the annual conference of the Society for Latin American Studies (Oxford, 1990).[1]

NOTE

1. For information about the seminar and its activities, please contact Mark Richmond, School of Social and Professional Studies, University of Humberside, Inglemire Avenue, Hull HU6 7LU. Tel: 0482 440550 ext. 4219. Fax: 0482 449624.

EUROPEAN NETWORK FOR RESEARCH ON LEARNING AND INSTRUCTION

Noel Entwistle

The European Network for Research on Learning and Instruction (EARLI) was established in 1985 "to promote the systematic exchange and discussion of ideas within the domain of instructional and educational research, as well as research on industrial training." It is a multidisciplinary society, but the membership reflects the predominant involvement of psychology departments in much of Europe in this area of research. In Britain, Holland, and the Scandinavian countries, education departments are much more involved in empirical research than elsewhere. Besides the countries of Western Europe, members are drawn from most of the Central and Eastern European countries, although currency problems mean that special arrangements have had to be made to encourage their involvement.

The founding of EARLI was made possible by financial support by the Dutch Council for Educational Research (SVO), which continued until the number of members enabled it to become self-sufficient. No help was forthcoming from the European Community (EC), in spite of considerable efforts to find such support. By now EARLI has over 750 members and has established an academic journal, *Learning and Instruction*, besides a newsletter, *EARLI News*, which has been produced regularly since 1986. Members also are invited to join one or more of fifteen special interest groups (SIGs) with the intention of creating groups of researchers who communicate regularly and promote collaborative research studies. Some of the SIGs have been lively and have circulated their own information, but it has proved difficult for the executive committee to ensure activity in all the groups. National correspondents have also been appointed to help in the networking of information, again with variable success.

The most successful work of EARLI to date has centered around the biennial conferences, which have been held in Leuven, Tubingen, Madrid, and Turku, with the fifth conference held in Aix-en-Provence in early September 1993. These conferences have proved an excellent way of promoting contact between researchers. It has proved much more difficult to encourage communication through the newsletter, and even the journal in its early stages, probably because of language difficulties. Although most EARLI members read English quite well, many are uncertain of their ability to write it correctly. This seems to be a continuing problem in establishing at least the formal parts of the network.

ACTIVITIES OF THE COMMITTEE ON EDUCATIONAL RESEARCH IN COOPERATION WITH THIRD WORLD COUNTRIES

Wolfgang Karcher

The Committee on Educational Research in Cooperation with Third World Countries has been in existence for fifteen years. It grew out of a dialogue between educational researchers and the German Foundation for International Development (DSE) and subsequently became a committee of the German Educational Research Association, with Prof. Dr. Dietrich Goldschmidt of the Max Planck Institute for Educational Research in Berlin as the founding chairman.

The committee is an amalgam of social scientists and research-oriented volunteers engaging in different ways with educational research in the Third World. In the old and new Federal Republic of Germany (FRG) we have merely one chair for this field (at the University of Frankfurt am Main). All other social researchers currently involved with this theme of study do so out of a personal interest within or along with their specialization. As a result, the motivation of the scientists to work in this field may be high but the possibilities of intensive study are limited. As diverse as its membership, is the relationship of the active committee members to scientific institutions in the Third World as well as to developmental organizations in Germany and in general to social issues and politics.

For a couple of years a critical connection between scientific research and political action seems to have prevailed. The general goals of the work of the committee are to critically accompany social developments and to give critical advice to developmental aid organizations. The committee is a component of the German Educational Research Association, in that it has an important role in observing educational research with regard to the Third World being conducted within the German-speaking context. Presently about 150 persons are connected with the committee.

A substantial part of the work of the committee consists of mutual exchange through seminars and symposiums and through the publication of a circular. The latter comprises news on the activities of the committee and on seminars and publications relevant to the theme of educational research. The seminars lay special emphasis on those themes which the committee members believe to be important and suitable for intensive discussions. They are held once or twice a year. Contributions are frequently published.

Every two years the committee takes part in a symposium together with another committee, the congress on the German Association for Educational Science. At the end of the 1970s the committee produced a first state-of-the-art report concerning publications in German on the theme of educational research in Third World countries.

In the backdrop of the German unification process of 1990, an exchange of experience and opinions with colleagues from the former German Democratic Republic (DDR) was organized. Also, during the years 1991 and 1992, discussions took place on the sector concept of the German Ministry of Economic Cooperation and Development with regard to different levels of the educational system in the context of bilateral aid. Comments on the new sector concept are currently being worked out.

A workshop on missionary pedagogy was organized in early 1992 at the Congress of the German Association for Educational Science. This was an attempt not only to bring to the fore a theme more or less forgotten, but to reflect on its present day implications.

The international dimension of the committee has had a sporadic character. In cooperation with its respective sister organizations, two international conferences were held a few years ago, first in Brighton, Great Britain and then in Wageningen, the Netherlands. The third was held in 1993 in Berlin with the theme, Education, Work and Sustainability in the South: Experiences and Strategies. The conference was organized in cooperation with the German Foundation for International Development. One-third of its participants came from countries of the South.

The committee is cautiously searching to strengthen its international relationships on a European level, which until now have been limited partly because communication has been in the German language. Contacts with persons from the South operate primarily on an individual basis, as the committee has very little financial means for meeting travel costs.

DSE'S EXPERIENCE
WITH NETWORKING AND
INSTITUTIONAL DEVELOPMENT

Wolfgang Gmelin

The German Foundation for International Development (DSE) is a private organization of German development assistance according to its statutes. However, as it is financed practically entirely out of the German government's development cooperation budget, it is in fact a specialized part of German development cooperation.

DSE's motto, Dialogue and Training, characterizes its specialization on the promotion of exchange of experience and the training of specialists and executives from developing countries, but it also shows its limitations. In spite of being called a foundation, DSE cannot fund.

DSE is organized in specialized departments, called centers: for agriculture, public administration, economic and social development, health, vocational education and training, and general and higher education.

In spite of the limitations of DSE's instruments they nevertheless permit certain points of entry to institution building through training, that is, the qualification of staff. The so-called dialogue facility of DSE, the open exchange of experiences among professionals, researchers, and policy decision makers had fulfilled functions of a network: a forum for reflecting on policy issues and alternatives, for reviewing and disseminating results, and for bringing together the research and the decision making process.

Over the past ten years, DSE has moved from more or less isolated program activities to longer term so-called program packages in which the different instruments of DSE are combined. The dialogue events serve for reflection and conceptional work, that are to establish basis for cooperation. But they also serve the needs assessment for training, the identification of resources available locally or in the region, and the need for external inputs. The dialogue events are also used for reviewing and monitoring cooperative training ventures. These short- and longer-term training programs of DSE are mostly specialized, tailor-made courses fitted into particular plans and activities of partner institutions. For example, if a curriculum development institute is facing a major revision of curricula or the introduction of a new subject, such specialized training could be agreed upon.

As a program package evolves, the planning and monitoring of the events should ideally become activities of the partner institution with DSE acting only as a facilitator providing information on experts and expertise from outside and making it available. Use of the DSE instrument, sending of experts/consultants, has been increasing during the past ten years. Partner institutions will ask DSE to provide certain resources/resource persons known to them or will help identify such expertise and make it available.

Another type of so-called "light instruments of involvement" is the congress support facility under which DSE can provide scholars and professionals from developing countries with support to attend scientific symposia and professional meetings abroad (e.g., in Germany or in a developing country other than the home country of the applicant).

The Education, Science, and Documentation Centre of DSE has had ever since its establishment in the early seventies a focus on basic school and out-of-school education in Africa. Given the limitation of DSE's instruments on training activities, it concentrated from the beginning on what were considered strategic points of entry to reforms of education systems, that is, curriculum development and evaluation, teaching materials, and in-service teacher training.

A major program in this area has been the cooperation with the African Curriculum Organization (ACO) on curriculum development in Africa. On the basis of an assessment of staff needs in African curriculum centers, a training program consisting of specialized intensive training courses at regional, subregional and national levels was conceived for the target groups of directors of curriculum development centers, professional staff of the centers, and experts associated with the work of curriculum centers. Parallel to these specially designed intensive training courses, DSE made available scholarships for degree programs at African universities. The evaluation of the program was conceived as a combination of the classical questionnaire and interview information gathering with a series of evaluation workshops at curriculum development centers, thus associating a large number of former participants in training events with evaluation exercise.

The African Curriculum Organization at its outset in 1975–76 had the ambition of becoming a network. In addition to the joint training activities with the DSE, a secretariat was to collect all pertinent information on curriculum development relevant for the member centers and to make it available upon request and through regular newsletters to the member centers. It also was to build up a roster of experts and was supposed to act as a clearing house in the field of curriculum development.

However, the network functioned mainly via the dialogue and training events organized in cooperation with DSE. Due to a general reluctance of donors to finance over a prolonged period of time the institutional ingredients for a network, that is to say, a qualified and continuously functioning secretariat, ACO could never provide the other services. Thus, it could not prove its worth to member centers. However, it is doubtful if the contributions in foreign currency of member institutions would have come in a sufficient amount if the services could have been provided.

In addition, there were certain built-in obstacles to the success of a regionwide network. The geographic scope with potentially all African countries was too wide. If a good deal of the networking had to be done by bringing people physically together, the network would be too expensive. For the time being the only activities seem to be national and subregional.

In DSE we have experience with a number of networks and associations formed after major international events. An example is the initiative of UNESCO Institute of Education in Hamburg in cooperation with DSE to ensure the follow-up of Jomtien recommendations by forming a network on evaluation of nonformal basic education programs. The project aims to develop information, monitoring, feed-back evaluation strategies, and to document and disseminate the experience gained in different settings. Documentation work and the need to get members of the network together occasionally requires considerable funding which the member organizations usually cannot muster.

Experience with the international task force on literacy formed by government organizations of adult education in the international literacy year, which was monitored by the International Council for Adult Education did function well as a clearing house for experiences, programs, and resource persons to be exchanged. However, the action plans developed became relevant almost exclusively for the individual organizations and did not lead to any major joint actions. These were hampered by various obstacles including rivalries between large organizations.

DSE also has experience with a number of smaller informal networks which developed out of multi-annual joint programs with a number of partner organizations. These networks mainly served the purpose of following up on the particular training activities, of keeping the participants informed on what is going on in their field, and of establishing professional links. Such informal networks have come into existence for distance educators in East Africa, and for other persons who have assisted in the information and documentation training activities sponsored by DSE. The vehicle is the newsletter *Information Trends* which goes to some 120 libraries in East and Southern Africa in addition to the participants in former DSE events.

In the field of higher education, DSE helped to create a rather original approach to university staff development in East and South Africa. Over a period of five years (1987–1992) a program which was originally relatively strongly driven from DSE gradually was taken over and appropriated by the members of the training program, that is, by staff developers from East and South African universities. The actual training became more and more oriented to the conditions and the needs of the participating universities. As the target group stabilized, its members developed plans for adapting teaching materials. The joint university-DSE program evolved into a network called the University Staff Development in Eastern and Southern Africa (USDESA) based at the University of Harare. There is still hope that the necessary coordinating secretariat work will find financial backing.

The latest of the DSE-sponsored networks is one to evolve out of a training program on qualitative empirical educational research. This program has been developed upon the request of partner institutions and is geared mainly to younger educational researchers in Kenya, Tanzania, and Uganda.[1] The core elements of this network are also a series of training and exchange-of-experience events for the same group of persons over a period of time, on-the-job consultancies between the various events by external and local facilitators, and the provision of materials and sharing of information through a newsletter. This program has the advantage of being embedded in the larger framework of ERNESA. The coordinator of the DSE-sponsored training activities is serving as the link to ERNESA and to other programs in the area sponsored by other donor organizations.

Such informal specialized networks geared to a particular program function well as long as there are ongoing activities with assured finance. Links to more formalized associations like ERNESA and, through ERNESA, to NORRAG provide backstopping and a chance for sustainability. As a matter of fact, the education research training program benefited from the outset and still is benefiting from NORRAG.

NOTE

1. See *NORRAG News* No. 14 for details.

SCOTTISH EDUCATION ACTION FOR DEVELOPMENT

Linda Gray

Scottish Education Action for Development (SEAD) focuses its work on issues of development which Scotland shares with countries of the so-called Third World. By first addressing problems in Scotland arising from poverty, powerlessness, injustice, and so on, it is possible to increase the interest and awareness of sectors of the adult Scottish population in the problems facing their counterparts overseas. One of the outcomes of this work is that closer links are developed between the counterparts not only in a South-North exchange but also in South-South and North-North connections. This is important because it is apparent that groups sharing the same area of concern, when in a country as small as Scotland, often have little or no awareness of each other's activities or experience.

In stimulating South-North contacts, SEAD places particular emphasis on just how much people in Scotland can learn from their opposite numbers in the world's poorest countries. The ultimate aim is to stimulate action for change. Some of the links established to date are between groups in Glasgow and Chile, Fife and South Africa, and Inverness and the Solomon Islands.[1]

NOTE

1. For more information contact SEAD, 23 Castle Street, Edinburgh EH2, UK

LATIN AMERICA

PART VII

There is a long history of educational research in Latin America. The modern period could be dated to the late 1950s, when educational planning came into vogue. Planners made heavy use of research first for purposes of diagnoses of problems, later for suggestions of strategies that might be effective. This led to the creation of a number of centers of research in governments, in universities, and in private settings.

Red Latinoamericana de Información y Documentación en Educación (REDUC) is not the only example of important accomplishments in research and networking in Latin America, but it is an important one. It brings together twenty-six research centers, public and private, located in fifteen countries. During its twenty years of work, REDUC and its member centers have generated more than 20,000 abstracts of research and writing on education in Latin America. Abstracts are available in microfiche and CD-ROM, and it is possible to obtain paper copies of original documents.

REDUC's problem, as discussed by Cariola, and later by Schiefelbein, has been how to make use of this enormous research. Various strategies have been tried, including meetings and conferences with decision makers invited, state-of-the-art reviews written about current policy issues, production of brief summaries or policy briefs that summarize in nontechnical language what we know about problems and ways to resolve them, and training programs for researchers, educators, and policy makers, often together.

Cariola concludes that all these efforts have had some effect, but less than desired. He is more impressed with the impact on education policy of newcomers to the field, professionals from other disciplines who have not been part of previous efforts at networking. Major policies in education are now taken on the basis of research by economists, outside the mainstream of education research.

Cariola sees this crossing of lines as favorable for education. Economists and managers from the business sector bring into education new perspectives that can regenerate creativity in education research and lead to solutions to problems that previously had puzzled us. He cites several examples of the intervention of the newcomers.

At the same time, Cariola argues, there is also increasing attention to a new perspective on knowledge. He distinguishes between knowledge presented as fact and knowledge generated in the process of activity, or representational knowledge as knowledge-as-skill. This distinction, made in other papers in this collection, suggests the value of linking conventional researchers with managers and practitioners to increase our understanding of processes in education.

In a second paper, Cariola summarizes lessons learned from REDUC's experience of attempting to increase utilization of scientific knowledge by decision makers. Among the conclusions he draws are the following:

1. It is not hard to build a database of educational research. The main requirements are a stable institution and a dedicated documentalist. In his chapter, Schiefelbein says that you also need a committed organizer and fund raiser.

2. Decision makers don't seek the kind of data researchers can present them. They don't read, and they may not understand the forms of presentation used by researchers to communicate to each other.

3. Decision makers do use information, however. They rely on "trusted advisors" who are both knowledgeable and speak the language of the decision maker.

Cariola also thinks that new technologies of communication may increase use of information by decision makers. This is more likely to the extent the technology presents information in familiar and accessible ways.

The chapter by González describes REDUC's most recent efforts in the use of computer technology to make research-based information available to decision makers and others. González has developed a computer-based simulation game similar to the more heuristic table game developed in the Basic Research and Implementation in Developing Education Systems Project (BRIDGES). He also has developed a system for rapid searching and organizing of text. His software program can in a few minutes read several hundred pages of text and develop an outline that tells the reader the major elements of content of the document. REDUC is developing other similar software programs intended to make it much easier for decision makers and others to query documents.

The critical question of these new techniques for communication will be, of course, the extent to which they contribute to communication between producers and users of information, and contribute directly to the process of information generation.

CULTURES OF POLICY, CULTURES OF RESEARCH IN LATIN AMERICA

Patricio Cariola, S.J.

In this chapter I, first, review the relationship between policy and research in the development of Latin American education; second, point at the basic changes occurring today in the culture of policy and research; and third, draw a few conclusions for networking between these two fields.

Latin American countries have a lot in common, more perhaps than any other region in the world, and they are very different at the same time. Public education systems have come through similar stages of development, but each stage differs greatly according to the time the state modernized. Countries can be organized into three types:

1. The Southern Cone countries and Costa Rica, where at the turn of the century you find an organized system of public primary and secondary schools, plus one or two state universities, built under the prevalent German influence. Policies were carefully designed and carried out, and the quality of education did not deteriorate until the great expansion of the 1960s and 1970s and the political and economic crisis of the 1980s.

2. The bigger countries like Venezuela, Colombia, Mexico, and to a great extent Brazil, which developed their systems in the 1920s and 1930s and began to grow exponentially after World War II. Here the influence was mostly from the United States. The systems expanded with great differences in quality. There was, however, a measure of planning.

3. The other countries in Central America and the Andean Region which have caught up with the rest enrollment-wise at the primary level, except in rural areas, in the 1980s. Here the influence was entirely from the United States. Quality was always difficult to achieve.

Problems affecting the organization and expansion of systems tend to become qualitatively similar as time goes on, although the institutional resources to tackle them, traditions and qualified personnel, continue to vary according to their historical development. So does the presence of research and its use in policy making today.

With these differences in view a few comments can be made on the development of the relationship between policy and research in the region as a whole.

A relation between policy and research did not exist until the late 1950s, when development theories and practices came onto the scene. Up to that point liberal ideology, political pressure from the middle classes, and general concern for progress had pushed forward the organization and expansion of education. Policy was inspired by European and United States education. It was finally a compromise between liberal and conservative parties, secularists and the Church.

The general concern of economists with planning, UNESCO's interest in educational planning, plus the general development of the social sciences paved the way for educational research. It was intended to help planning. It was basically quantitative and related to a decision to expand the system. It was done in ministries of education and planning and in schools of economics and sociology. It was used to produce plans for the ministries and projects to obtain foreign aid, and was to be simple research for simple policy decisions. When it came to decisions having to do with quality, a few national and foreign experts were called in.

Educational research matured and developed in the 1970s, but rather independently of policy decisions. Planning offices lost importance or perhaps planning had become part of decision making. The Ford Foundation and the U.S. Agency for International Development assisted the development of research, in ministries, universities, and in the independent research centers that began to appear. But the effort succeeded only in fairly autonomous university units and in the independent centers.

Two other phenomena conspired to widen the gap between research and policy cultures. One was the impact of the "reproduction theories" which made researchers particularly critical of the school system. The other was the repressive regimes of the 1970s and 1980s which either closed their doors to, or alienated, social and educational researchers.

These developments interacted with each other to produce significant innovations in nonformal education. This in turn has produced learning that is quite useful in thinking about and coming up with new means of improving quality in school as a whole. On the other hand, international cooperation concentrated its efforts on nongovernmental institutions, among them educational research centers. Although distanced from national policy making, these groups were closely connected through regional networks—UNESCO, Latin American Council for the Study of Social Sciences (CLACSO), REDUC, Latin American Regional Center for Literacy and Adult Education (CREFAL)—plus groups specializing in qualitative research, education and work, and early childhood.

Work in the centers and regional networking has been particularly productive in shaping regional diagnostics and policies and in preparing decision makers and especially qualified technical personnel for the democratic governments that replaced authoritarian ones.

The basic contribution of research has been to reinforce and ground the generalized conviction that public education systems have either lost their original quality or whatever quality they managed to achieve, according to the conditions in which the systems developed.

Quality, understood as pertinence, effectiveness, and equity in learning, is now the issue for governments and regional organizations. It is becoming more and more a national issue in every country. Policies that are being adopted have a great deal to do with the work of researchers during the last decade or so in the institutions mentioned. Exile from policy making, both intellectual and political, has curiously born fruits for policy. In this sense the 1980s, the lost decade for Latin America, has not been entirely lost.

As these developments went on in the culture of research, governments in one way or another began to decentralize and privatize schools during the 1980s as part of structural adjustment policies. No researcher would have ever dreamed of such a thing, only a conservative economist. Policies came from outside the field of education, especially from economists.

The extent and impact of decentralization and privatization of costs differ according to countries. In some the policies have been drastic, in others not, but all are moving in the same direction. Little has been written about this issue: researchers are just beginning to assess the consequences, particularly in terms of quality.

Changes in the political economy worldwide have helped to integrate decentralization with the other ideas for reform in the region. Probably the best example of a proposal that pulls together the efforts of researchers and the need to compete in a global market is the Economic Commission for Latin America (CEPAL)–UNESCO report of 1992. In fact it is the result of research couched in language that speaks to economists and business people. It could be called "education and development in Latin America revisited."

The seminar, La Investigacion Latinoamericana de cara al año 2000 (Punta de Tralca, May 1993), called by CLACSO and REDUC to produce an agenda for educational research, is another example of this trend from the point of view of content, participants, and organization. The basic points of the agenda are the demands of the economy, society, and culture today; management and financing of decentralized systems and effective learning, particularly in the early grades. Half of the participants were active researchers, the other half were researchers in top policy positions in ministries or development agencies. The seminar was piggybacked on the biannual regional conference to promote education organized by UNESCO (in good RRAG tradition!). Conclusions were introduced and distributed on the floor of the conference and the whole subject of research in relation to policy decisions permeated the discussions and conclusions. Many of the participants in the seminar were delegation members or had been invited to attend the conference.

A number of advances were made in 1994. The ministry in Argentina organized a seminar on changes in secondary education with researchers from neighboring countries. In Chile groups of researchers competed with proposals for thirteen studies on the same subject. Bolivia created a network of researchers to do studies for the government. In Mexico a private research center, the Centro de Estudio Educativos, devised a model using ministry and census information to group municipalities, and schools within them, according to scholastic performance. The center is selling the model to the federal states, together with advice on policies to improve efficiency and equity within those states. In Belo Horizonte, Brazil, the secretary of education had as his advisor one of the principal educational researchers in the country, who, in turn, had been head of the educational system of the city of Sao Paulo.

CHANGES IN THE CULTURE OF POLICY

The basic changes in the culture of policy making seem to be, one, the growing weight of ministries of finance in decisions having to do with financing and administration; and two, the more active role of specialists, researchers, and research in more educational decisions, as just seen.

Introducing expertise and research in ministries, however, is not easy. A cultural clash takes place between the new criteria and procedures based on research and the established ones based on experience; between social scientists coming from NGOs, and teachers coming from the educational system. This tension has crossed party lines within the government coalition. It is more a question of fields than of politics. In some countries the problem is how to attract high-level professionals to work in ministries. Low salaries, instability, and frustration with politics turn out to be powerful deterrents. Also from this point of view, foreign loans can be of help. They can allow for better salaries, professional development, and a measure of stability.

Rather than change, one could speak of a direction in which things begin to move when it comes to a closer connection between research and research results. But again things differ from one country to another. More significant changes are taking place in the culture of research.

CHANGES IN THE CULTURE OF RESEARCH

Looking at research from the vantage point of REDUC (Latin American Network of Education Research Centers), we notice a clear diminution of substantial research programs and projects in the region, with the exceptions mentioned above. Agencies and foundations have made severe cuts in research. There is precious little basic research going on, if we can distinguish this from more focused strictly policy-oriented programs. It is even true in nonformal education where there was so much creativity in years gone by. It is happening in social science as a whole.

On the other hand, the educational research centers that managed to institutionalize in the 1970s keep active and renew their personnel, even though there is a question mark as to how they will evolve in the future.

In terms of use of this research REDUC has managed to collect research results in every country in the region; this is "the first floor," the "second floor" is the use of research.

Jose Joaquin Brunner made use of research the subject of his opening address at the recent (1993) Punta de Tralca seminar. After discussing the growing limitations of standard concepts of using research results in an increasingly interactive process of decision making where decisions muddle through, moved by a diversity of agents, each self-propelled by his own interest, he suggested that instead of considering the representative side of knowledge (its symbolic nature) we should concentrate on

> knowledge as dispositions and skills that allow its possessor an informed behavior, a specific practice. Knowledge-as-representation intends, above all, to communicate and obtain recognition from other producers within the respective disciplinary communities. Knowledge-as-skill is practiced and its use determined by a structure of opportunities that is always closer to the action pole and decisions than to the pole of production. (p. 10)

In my opinion, this view of knowledge better accounts for the way knowledge is used today in Latin America and for the role of researchers in ministries, banks, foundations, business organizations concerned with education, as well as research positions. It also accounts for the needs as they are actually perceived by people in policy. One of them, a former researcher, once told me, "What we need is a REDUC with two legs," meaning a person who knew how to use its contents in specific situations.

Brunner borrows from Reich (1991) the concept of symbolic analysts, together with routine production services and personal services as one of the three basic occupations of the future, to describe this new role of social researchers as a whole.

Symbolic analysts (1) identify, solve, or act as mediators through the manipulation of symbols and use analytic instruments, (2) receive income not linked to time-on-task but to *the contribution their services actually make*, and (3) have professional careers that are not lineal, but instead dependent on their capacity to deliver, the prestige they manage to accumulate, and their participation in networks and teams of specialists.

The role of researchers as producers of research for use by third parties seems to be changing quickly. The market needs people who can produce, identify, and apply knowledge in a variety of situations; people who have the competence to deliver what is truly needed. In other words, the distance between production and use of knowledge seems to be shortening, as if the skills side of knowledge have begun to mean more than the representative one. In this sense, researchers secluded in university departments seem to be in a clear disadvantage with regard to think tanks, private consulting offices, legislative consultants, different policy analysis agencies, and networks of symbolic analysts who connect themselves loosely with an expanding market for services manipulating knowledge. Globalization of markets has a lot to do with the situation.

This new way of speaking about use of knowledge is closely related to that of circuit riders (Myers, 1981), brokers, or policy analysts. The ideas and techniques developed by BRIDGES seem to be particularly adequate to train researchers and planners. In this sense, the Brunner paper confirmed the decision made to make use of BRIDGES to build a "second floor" to REDUC.

CONSEQUENCES FOR NETWORKING

Three consequences for networking, as understood in the RRAG tradition, occur to me. The first is the need to include, and privilege, economists specializing in social policy in the business of networking in education. Evolution in the culture of policy making in education only confirms the importance of their position and the roles they play in it. We need to learn each other's language and understand each other's concerns. Something similar should be said about including business leaders sensitive to education and training problems. Education has all to gain from closer connections with business and symbolic analysts in economics, inside and outside the government. And so does the economy. The really new thing about economists and business people is the role they assign to education as markets and competition globalize. They are not willing to spend less, but more. They want to be convinced on how to do it. At least such is the discourse.

The second is the close connection between the concept of networking and that of the symbolic analyst as described by Reich and Brunner. Both seem to respond to similar ways of understanding present needs of relating knowledge to action, to a certain way of being in the world, to the current integration and globalization of cultural processes. In that sense they belong to the same family of concepts. Networking would seem to be the typical activity of a symbolic analyst. The emphasis is on communication, on the capacity to listen and to tap the information necessary to respond adequately in a specific situation.

The third is the need for national, regional, and international networking. In order to become competitive, countries need the best information and expertise, wherever it can be found. Symbolic analysts need not only results of research (in the form of state-of-the-art reviews), more or less analyzed, but also reviews of the state-of-the-practice. They need quantitative information, who's who, results of important meetings, new policies and projects, and computer programs. Databases have to be interconnected and e-mail used for personal contact and transmission of data.

LESSONS LEARNED
FROM REDUC (1972–1992)

Patricio Cariola, S.J.

From the outset, REDUC (a network of linked institutions that produce abstracts of education research in Latin America)[1] was not intended as a purely documentary or academic exercise. The idea was always to inform decision making. We have succeeded in building a database of 20,000 abstracts through a cooperative network of centers in seventeen countries. However, our achievements in terms of use of the products of REDUC by people in decision-making positions, and even by academics, are far more modest. We can tell a number of stories about the impact of REDUC, but we cannot speak of widespread use. But the target and the dream (impossible?) are there. Here are some lessons we have learned in an effort to make those dreams come true.

It is one thing to collect and make information available. It is a very different thing to dish it out in a way that is useful to decision makers in their every day practice. It is unusual for decision makers to use "fresh" knowledge in their practice. In this business, therefore, you have to work more on the demand side than on the supply side. The real challenge in the use of knowledge is not technical, organizational, or financial. It is cultural.

People in planning, policy making, and administration are just beginning to realize that they have to read. But the pressures coming from current breakdowns of educational systems are not of the kind that force them to scan regional or world experience in order to find ways to tackle them. People trained in other disciplines search in the literature to find solutions to their problems. This is rare among us educationalists. We think we know the answers.

When it comes to their advisors, on the other hand, like the old parish priest, they would rather have people who have done their reading. That is because even when they are aware of the importance of seeking information, the truly friendly ways of accessing information are not so friendly. One frequently called advisor (who had worked for REDUC) told me "what we need here are two-legged

REDUCs." That is, we need brokers, people who can assimilate the contents of REDUC and then provide answers to current problems. We need, if you will, people who can both read and speak.

Just having REDUC available does not lead professors of education to use it, either. It is mostly used by researchers writing regional papers for development agencies or publication or by doctoral students writing dissertations for universities in the North.

One could trace this lack of a habit of using current, local, knowledge to schools of education and to the general weakness of education as an organized body of knowledge which if assessed, can produce differences in practice. This is not only a problem in the South, of course.

The doctoral program in educational research set up by Miguel Petty at the Catholic University of Cordoba in Argentina uses REDUC as its main source of bibliography. At the licentiate level, students are taught to abstract and write state-of-the-art papers using REDUC guidelines. Graduate students from other schools of education in town use the microfiches of the originals, plus the abstracts. This well-established experience shows that new habits can be created within training institutions that bear fruit later when graduates have to face real problems.

It is relatively easy to set up an operation like REDUC strictly from the angle of an up-to-date database if the following conditions are met: (1) An institution can be found whose interests are compatible with such an operation. The more it serves these interests, the greater the financial and general institutional support will be; and (2) The coordinating center manages to involve the other national centers in some sort of cooperative design and control of the operation and, secondly, obtains the resources to provide the various centers with the basic equipment, training, and minimal contribution to running expenses. As far as local contributions are concerned, experience shows that public institutions can assign personnel more easily, but usually fall behind private ones in terms of dissemination and general initiative. Heads of institutions are key actors in this regard.

At the operational level REDUC, as a database, is based on the dedication of documentalists. In every center you will find a documentalist for whom REDUC is more than just a job. The biannual meetings of directors and documentalists, plus joint training, forge close professional bonds and dedication. This is a network.

The real problems start when you try to bring the database to bear on decision making. This implies making your own the problems of those preparing actual decisions and acting as a broker between the data and the problem. This implies analysis and a different sort of professional than the traditional documentalist. You need people who can, through the intermediation of written texts and on the basis of the work of documentalists, set up a communications process, a conversation between researchers and people in ministries and school systems, and vice versa. Most persons still have a very mechanistic understanding of the information/decision-making process. There is little attention given to such factors as commitment and interpretation, capacity to listen to breakdowns and new distinctions, or to creativity.

Finally, every solution is a creation, not just an application of information. Information can trigger creativity; it won't replace it. We have learned this from communication theory, common sense, and practice.

Emphasis on "use" is not only an ethical imperative but also a practical one. International money is available to set up information systems and to introduce new technology, it is not just to keep databases up to date. There is a growing interest, however, in their use by policy people.

We are learning that such use can be increased by introducing intelligence into a database, that is, technology that makes it friendly, and by training brokers and users. [Ed. note: The chapter by González addresses this issue.] Training to become brokers and users seems to overlap with current methods to train in policy planning, and administration is constructed more and more as use of information.

Collecting, abstracting, and disseminating is a simple way to build up educational research even in the least developed contexts. It's a good starting point for more sophisticated stages in terms of use in practice and actual production of new research. But there must be leadership to make the difficult move from collecting to analyzing to dialogue with decision makers.

A final and obvious lesson is that although policy making and management have their own logic, the growing demand for efficiency and pertinence of social services (education particularly) makes it necessary to establish dynamic links between them. This is the business of databases, information (we would rather speak of communications) systems and networks. Working with REDUC has taught us that there is a growing demand to step up efforts in this direction. There are new frontiers, and new dreams.

NOTE

1. See Appendix 2 for a list of member research centers.

INCREASING NETWORK EFFECTIVENESS THROUGH TECHNOLOGY

José González Cornejo

THE FRAMEWORK OF REDUC ACTIVITIES AND MODEL

Over the past years REDUC has introduced technological innovations and systematic information treatment for collection, analysis, processing, and dissemination. It has developed the following process model for assisting query refinement using its online information retrieval system (see Figure 4).

REDUC implements this model by ensuring that users can conveniently access the system; once inside, researchers and policy makers may obtain information by using a semantic network of concepts within the same work environment. The enormous flow of information that can be made available and integrated through REDUC by means of computer enquiries means that the search generates more questions than it has answered. There is thus a corresponding need to develop efficient software which enables interaction with these hardware innovations. Software has been developed which has the capacity to read, write, or manipulate information from the high-capacity storage medium, and also allows electronic communication of this information among different users, either through local area networks or through telephone lines. This duality between hardware and software developments stimulated by the unprecedented information management demands placed on computer technologies has also fostered innovations in a procedure called hypertext which permits innovation in the collecting and analysis of educational research with respect to classification criteria, electronic storage of data, and creation of a network of links between text. CD-ROM, WORM, and scanner technology with optical recognition of text and telecommunication are all part of this.

These developments, combined with hypertext, permit us to surpass limitations of the classical forms of bibliographical databases which consist of publication data and abstracts. The new technologies make possible the use of full text capabilities.

Figure 4
A Model for Information Retrieval

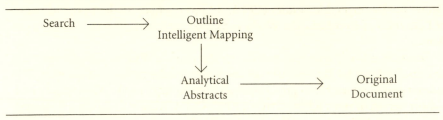

Source: González, 1992

After a user has completed a standard bibliographical search, the full text or portions of text could be read on the terminal screen, further analyzed with hypertext software, printed, filed, or converted to word processing format.

Applications Developed by REDUC

Hypertext. The complete database of REDUC is functioning in hypertext IZE. In other words, all 20,000 abstracts of REDUC have been loaded on a CD-ROM disk, and software has been written that permits full searching of the text. A publication on hypertext and its use in the documental treatment of data represents the state of practice of this retrieval information technology in REDUC. Research with the support of IDRC is underway to test and implement representative prototypes of hypertext applications and to generate a guide to information makers/users of databases. We currently are designing a system which facilitates the transition to building and retrieving the information from a hypertext concept point of view.

Causal model-analysis and simulation games. REDUC together with BRIDGES of Harvard University has carried out several workshops to improve use of research in policy making in Chile and Honduras. The workshops are run using specially designed training modules that can be carried to any setting. The modules were constructed using REDUC and RRAG approaches to research compilation and synthesis.

These modules introduce microcomputer software tools which can aid decision makers in understanding the relationships between educational goals. To adapt these modules to the Latin American situation, REDUC has designed DESAFIO, a group game based on a mathematical simulation cause-and-effect model[1] with a computer interface. DESAFIO provides easy access to documental and statistical databases. The simulation uses a table game, fictitious money, and a PC compatible, with a printer. Participants consist of a group of five or six people, which emulates a ministerial team. The generic objectives of DESAFIO are to stimulate the decision maker to consult researches in the field of education; provide training assistance through innovative instructional procedures; and provide a practical workshop leading toward practical solutions. The specific case scenario of the simulation is to increase coverage of secondary enrollment in Chile; and to improve the quality of teaching, efficiency of the system, and overall facilities. DESAFIO has been used in several workshops and demonstrations, with the Ministry of Education, Santiago, Chile, Economic Commission for Latin America (CEPAL) and Latin American Center for Demographic Studies (CELADE) postgraduate students, the Ministry of Education of Honduras, the World Bank, and the Interamerican Development Bank.

Semantic network system, automatic content analysis. REDUC has developed a universal indexer for the treatment of documental information in education. The indexer makes it possible to present the contents of large bodies of text to users in a short period of time. REDUC with CEPAL-CELADE have designed a hypertext data model in IZE to contain material downloaded from computer conferences or other electronic events. Software, a CoSy mapping program, has been developed: it is a computer program written specifically for the treatment of stored text files, within a methodological framework. The CoSy mapping program provides a mechanism for systematically tracing the evolution of transmitted messages covering CoSy issues.

Telecommunication. REDUC participated in a satellite project of NASA (Advanced Communication Technology Satellite), directed by Georgetown University.

NOTE

1. Based on a LISREL approach to causal modeling and nonexperimental research.

REDUC IN RELATION TO
OTHER LATIN AMERICAN NETWORKS

Ernesto Schiefelbein

A dozen of the many efforts carried out in Latin America to operate networks in education have succeeded for some time but only one has lasted for almost two decades in terms of exchanging information. Given the paucity of resources, networking has been the result of a financing sponsor rather than local efforts. Therefore, the networks operate as a result of the activity from the hub and little happens between the rest of the network members.

The Organization of American States (OAS), IDB–Brookings Foundation, and Ford Foundation during the 1970s; the International Development Research Centre (IDRC) from the 1970s to the 1990s; UNICEF, UNESCO, and the World Bank during the 1980s and 1990s; the Iberoamerican Education Organization (OEI) in the 1990s; and the Regional Office for Latin America of the International Labour Office (CINTERFOR-ILO) throughout the period have developed specialized networks. Each of these agencies has distributed some type of newsletter on each of the topics (research, production functions, adult education, training, preschooling, planning, or teacher training), convened seminars from time to time, and published the proceedings or selected papers produced by network members. The World Bank has also been using some of this data for their sectoral reports and project preparation.

In each case, once the hub has no longer been able to fund a joint research project or to keep mailing a newsletter, the network collapsed. It has taken a long time to realize that there is little money for exchanges and few local rewards for the scholarly work. The networks related to one person have been more resilient; for example, the UNICEF-Myers network in preschool education and the Maria Antonia Gallart network in training and employment. The failure of the Van Leer–Arango attempt may be explained by the violence and turmoil in Colombia rather than by the type of networking model.

REDUC has been able to operate and survive more than a decade given the low-cost strategies and cooperative structure built into the network, but the role of Patricio Cariola has been paramount in its survival and management. Over two-thirds of the cost is borne by the local centers, but the locus of control is in the region. Exchanges are made directly among the member centers, and the hub in Chile only produces the annual index of abstracts and the joint regional computer file.

However, the recent effort at sharing responsibilities among member centers will be a tough test of its endurance. REDUC has been able to include reports produced by networks no longer in operation and to coordinate efforts with specialized active networks such as CINTERFOR-ILO (Montevideo), IDRC, the Center for Trade Union Education, Latin America and Caribbean (CRESALC [UNESCO-Caracas]), the UNESCO networks for Central America, adult education (REDALF), planning (REPLAD), and teacher training (PICPEMCE), and in a lesser degree with OAS and the International Bureau of Education (IBE). Now that OEI is developing several databases there is once again the question whether there will be a cooperative or competitive relationship among the networks.

REDUC has been recently playing a key role in providing services to other networks. For example, planners send their research and reports to the local REDUC center and an abstract is produced. The abstract is published during the next four to six months by the local center and indexed in the regional REDUC Index. From time to time the specialized REPLAD network can retrieve all materials related with planning and publish a specialized issue with all abstracts and indexes by extracting the suitable materials from the REDUC mail files. Therefore, costs for each specialized network are reduced to printing and mailing, allowing the network to focus on exchanges and substantive matters. It is an interesting arrangement because it reduces interference with other networks, but allows sharing of efforts.

APPENDIX 1

CONTACT PERSONS AND ORGANIZATIONS IN THE SEARRAG NETWORK

Arfah Aziz
Teacher Education Division
Ministry of Education
Damansara Town Center
Kuala Lumpur
Malaysia

Prof. Zainal Ghani
Unit of Research in Basic Education
University Sains Malaysia
11800 Penang
Malaysia

Prof. Sim Wong Kooi
Centre for Applied Research in Education
National Institute of Education
Nanyang Technological University
469 Bukit Timah Road
Singapore

Dr. S. Gopinathan
Dept. of Comparative Education
National Institute of Education
Nanyang Technological University
469 Bukit Timah Road
Singapore

Mr. John Yip
Director of Education
Ministry of Education
Kay Siang Road
Singapore

Prof. Setiadji
Universitas Terbuka Indonesia
Pondok Cabe, Ciputat
Jakarta, Kotak Pos 6666
Indonesia

Dr. Aria Jalil
Director of Research
Universitas Terbuka Indonesia
Pondok Cabe, Ciputat
Jakarta, Kotak Pos 6666
Indonesia

Suheru Muljoatmodjo
Office of Ed. & Cultural Res. & Devt.
Ministry of Education and Culture
Jalan Jend. Sudirman,
Senayan, Jakarta
Indonesia

Dr. Pote Sapianchai
Ministry of University Affairs
238 Ayuthaya Road, Phya Thai
Bangkok 10400
Thailand

Dr. Wichai Tunsiri
Secretary General
National Education Commission
Sukhotai Road, Dusit
Bangkok
Thailand

Dr. Panom Pongpaibool
Director General
Curriculum and Instructional Devt. Centre
Ministry of Education
Bangkok
Thailand

Datuk Abd Bakar Apong
Vice Chancellor
Universiti Brunei Durassalam
Bandar Seri Begawan
Brunei Durassalam

Datuk Abd Razak Mohammad
Permanent Sec. & Director of Ed.
Ministry of Education
Bandar Seri Begawan
Brunei Durassalam

Dr. Mona Valisno
Bureau of Higher Education
DECS Complex
Meralco Ave, Pasig
Metro Manila
Philippines

Dr. Nilos Rosas
Director Regional DECS
Darang Misamil, Bago Bantal
Curzon
Philippines

Dr. Ramon Salinas, O.P.
Philippine Assn. for Graduate Ed.
Letran College, Intramuros
P. O. Box 146
Manila
Philippines

APPENDIX 2
ORGANIZATIONS
IN THE REDUC NETWORK

Name of Center: CIPES (Centro de Investigacion y Promocion Educativa y Social)
Contact Person: Dr. Luis Rigal, Director
Fax: (54–1) 786–0344
Telephone: (54–1) 784–3466
Address: Zabala 2677, 1426 Buenos Aires, Argentina

Name of Center: Universidad Catolica de Cordoba (UCC) Facultad de Filosofia
                    y Humanidades
Contact Person: Dr. Miguel Petty, S.J., Secretario de Ciencia y Tecnologia UCC;
                    Director Proyecto REDUC/UCC
Fax: (54–51) 241302
Telephone: (54–51) 238389
Address: Obispo Trejo 323, Piso, 5000 Cordoba, Argentina

Name of Center: CEBIAE (Centro Boliviano de Investigacion y Accion Educativa)
Contact Person: Dr. Jose Subirats, Director
Fax: (591–2) 372372
Telephone: (591–2) 342668
Address: Calle Hnos. Manchego 2518, La Paz, Bolivia

Name of Center: Fundacion Carlos Chagas
Contact Person: Sra. Maria da Graca Camargo Vieira,
                    Coordinadora F C Ch/REDUC
Fax: (55–11) 815–1059
Telephone: (55–11) 813–4511
Address: Av. Prof. Francisco Morato 1565, 05513 Sao Paulo, Brasil

Name of Center: INEP (Instituto Nacional de Estudos e Pesquisas Educacionais)
Contact Person: Sra. Marisa Perrone C Rocha, (SIBE); Coordinadora INEP/REDUC
Fax: (55–61) 347–8270
Telephone: (55–61) 347–8970
Address: Campus da Universidade de Brasilia, UnB, Asa Norte—Ala Sul,
                    Brasilia, DF, CEP: 70910

Name of Center: CIUP (Centro de Investigaciones, Universidad Pedagogica Nacional
Contact Person: Sra. Gloria Calvo, Coordinadora CIUP/REDUC
Fax: (571) 211–1293
Telephone: (571) 616–6512
Address: Calle 127 No. 12 A 20, Bogota, DE, Colombia

Name of Center: CINDE (Centro Internacional de Educacion y Desarrollo Humano)
Contact Person: Sra. Maria Cristina Garcia de Arango, Directora
Fax: (571) 218–7598
Telephone: (571) 256–4116
Address: Carrera 33 No. 91–50, La Castellana, Bogota, Colombia

Name of Center: CEMIE (Centro Multinacional de Investigacion Educativa)
                    Ministerio de Educacion Publica
Contact Person: Sra. Zaida Sanchez Moya, Directora CEMIE
Fax: (506) 552868
Telephone: (506) 224931
Address: Ministerio de Educacion Publica, Edificio Raventos, Piso 6,
                    San Jose, Costa Rica

Name of Center: ED-UCA (Universidad Centroamericana Jose Simeon Canas)
                    Instituto de Ciencias de la Educacion
Contact Person: Sr. Jose Luis Guzman, Coordinador REDUC/ED-UCA
Fax: (503)733384–731010
Telephone: (503) 734400 (Ext. 236)
Address: Autopista Sur, San Salvador, El Salvador, C. A.

Name of Center: CINDEG (Centro de Investigacion y Documentacion de Guatemala)
                    Universidad Rafael Landivar
Contact Person: Lcda Maria Luisa Escobar de Gomez, Coordinadora
                    REDUC/CINDEG
Fax: (502–2) 692756
Telephone: (502–2) 692151
Address: Campus de Vista Hermosa III, Zona 16, Guatemala

Name of Center: CIRE (Centro de Informacion y Recursos Educativos)
                    Universidad Pedagogica Nacional "Francisco Morazan,"
                    Depto de Recursos de Aprendizaje
Contact Person: Prof. Elizabeth Bendana de Toro, Directora CIRE
Fax: (504) 311257
Telephone: (504) 328037
Address: Boulevard Miraflores, Tegucigalpa D C, Honduras

Name of Center:	CEE (Centro de Estudios Educativos
Contact Person:	Lcdo Rolando Maggi, Coordinador REDUC/CEE
Fax:	(525) 664–3039
Telephone:	(525) 593–5776
Address:	Av Revolucion 1291, Col San Angel, Tlacopac, Del Alvaro Obergon, 01040 Mexico D F, Mexico

Name of Center:	CREFAL (Centro de Cooperacion Regional para la Educacion de Adultos en America Latina y el Caribe
Contact Person:	Dr. Mario Aguilera Dorantes, Director
Fax:	(52–454) 20092
Telephone:	(52–454) 21898
Address:	Quinta Erendira s/n, Patzcuaro, MICH 61600 Mexico

Name of Center:	MED (Ministerio de Educacion) Division General de Planificacion, Oficina de Investigacion y Documentacion
Contact Person:	Lcda Maria Teresa de Bendana, Secretaria Gral. del MED
Fax:	(505–2) 50698
Telephone:	(505–2) 50195
Address:	Complejo Civico "Camilo Ortega S" Modulo K, Managua, Nicaragua

Name of Center:	ICASE (Instituto Centroamericano de Administracion y Supervision de la Educacion)
Contact Person:	Dr. Nestor Porcell, Director
Fax:	(507) 649854
Telephone:	(507) 642586
Address:	Universidad de Panama, Estafeta Universitaria Panama, R de Panama

Name of Center:	CPES (Centro Paraguayo de Estudios Sociologicos)
Contact Person:	Dr. Domingo Rivarola, Director
Fax:	(595–21) 447128
Telephone:	(595–21) 443734
Address:	Eligio Ayala 973, Asuncion, Paraguay

Name of Center:	INIDE (Instituto Nacional de Investigacion y Desarrollo de la Educacion)
Contact Person:	Dr. Cesar Vigo Vargas, Director General
Fax:	(51–14) 360707
Telephone:	(51–14) 364990
Address:	Jr. Van de Velde 160, San Borja, Lima 100 Peru

Name of Center:	Centro de Estudios y Promocion del Desarrollo
Contact Person:	Sr. Luis Miguel Saravia Canales, Presidente
Fax:	(51–14) 617309
Telephone:	(51–14) 627193
Address:	Leon de la Fuente No. 110, Lima 17, Peru

Name of Center: CEDIE (Centro de Documentacion en Informacion Educativa) Universidad Catolica Madre Y Maestra
Contact Person: Lcda Amarilis Perez de Zapata, Directora CEDIE
Fax: (1–809) 581–7750
Telephone: (1–809) 581–6246
Address: Autopista Duarte Km 1 1/2, Santiago de los Caballeros, Republica Dominicana

Name of Center: CIEP (Centro de Investigacion y Experimentacion Pedagogica)
Contact Person: Dr. Waldo Warren, Director
Fax: (598–2) 983873
Telephone: (598–2) 983868
Address: 18 de Julio 965, Piso 3, Montevideo 11.100 Uruguay

Name of Center: CINTERFOR (Centro Interamericano de Investigacion y Documentacion sobre Formacion Profesional)
Contact Person: Lcda Martha Piaggio, Jefe Servicio de Documentacion e Informacion, Coordinador REDUC/CINTERFOR
Fax: (598–2) 223591
Telephone: (598–2) 986023
Address: Av Uruguay 1238, Montevideo, Uruguay

Name of Center: Ministerio de Educacion y Cultura
Contact Person: Prof. Rodolfo Gonzalez Rissoto, Director de Ed
Address: Reconquista 535, Piso 6, Montevideo, Uruguay

Name of Center: CERPE (Centro de Reflexion y Planificacion Educativa)
Contact Person: Dr. Luis Basabe, S.J., Director
Telephone: (582) 461–1505
Address: Avenida Santa Teresa de Jesus, Edificio CERPE, La Castellana, Caracas 1060–A, Venezuela

Name of Center: UNESCO/CRESALC (Centro Regional para la Educacion Superior en America Latina y el Caribe)
Contact Person: Lcda Monica Rothgaenger de Rivera, Directora SID/CRESALC/REDUC
Fax: (582) 262–0428
Telephone: (582) 284–5075
Address: 7a Avenida, entre 7a y 8a Transversales Altamira, Caracas 1062–A, Venezuela

APPENDIX 3

A PARTIAL LISTING OF NEWSLETTERS

ABEL Information Bulletin, AED, 1255 23rd St. NW, Washington, D.C. 20037

AERN Newsletter, Ohio University Libraries, Ohio University, Athens, OH 45701

African Forum for Children's Literacy in Science and Technology, newsletter, 13 floor Intl. House, Box 47543, Nairobi, Kenya

BCIES Newsletter, David Turner, 113 Princes Avenue, Palmers Green, London N13 6EH, U.K. (Contact for e-mail newsletter link initiative: david14@uk.ac.uel.bkmain or david14@bkmain.uel.ac.uk)

Bernard van Leer Newsletter, Box 82334, 2508 EH, The Hague, Netherlands

Bildungsforschung mit der dritten Welt, Tech. Univ. Berlin, FB 22,FR 4-8, Franklinstr, 28-29, D-1000 Berlin, Germany

CAETA Newsletter, c/o Dept. of Continuing Educ., Univ. Of Warwick, Coventry CV4 7AL, U.K.

CIESC Newsletter, Humanities Dept., CEGEP John Abbot College, Box 2000, Quebec H9X 3L9, Canada (Comp. Ed. Soc. of Canada)

ComLearn, 1700–777 Dunsmuir St., Box 10428 Pacific Centre, Vancouver BC, V7Y 1K4, Canada

Coordinator's Notebook, UNICEF, 3 UN Plaza, New York, NY 10017

Cultures and Development, 174 rue Joseph II, B-1040, Brussels, Belgium

DSA-Forum, newsletter of the Development Studies Association (U.K.), c/o IDPM, University Precinct Centre, University of Manchester, Manchester M13 9QS, U.K.

EADI Newsletter, Box 272 1211 Geneva 21, Switzerland

EARLI News, Department of Education, University of Edinburgh, 10 Buccleuch Place, Edinburgh, EH8 9JT, Scotland

Education News, Room 1156 UNICEF, 3 UN Plaza, New York, NY 10017

Education & Training, Task Force, Human Resources, Education and Training, Com. of Eur. Comm., 200 rue de la Loi, B-1049, Brussels, Belgium

Education y Trabajo, CENEP, Casilla 4397, 1000 Buenos Aires, Argentina

Educational Innovation and Information, IBE, Box 199, CH 1211 Geneva 20, Switzerland

EFA 2000, EFA Secretariat, UNESCO, 7 place de Fontenoy, Paris 75700, France

ERNESA Newsletter, Fac. of Education, Univ. of Dar es Salaam, Box 35048, Dar es Salaam, Tanzania

ERNWACA News, c/o W. Rideout, University of Southern California, Los Angeles, CA

The Forum for Advancing Basic Education & Literacy, HIID, One Eliot St., Cambridge, MA 01238

HMT Bulletin, 107–109 Temple Chambers, Temple Av., London EC4Y ODT, U.K.

ICAE News, 720 Bathurst St., Suite 500, Toronto, M5S 2R4, Canada

IIEP Newsletter, 7–9 rue Eugène Delacroix, Paris 75116, France

INED Newsletter, IBE, Box 199, CH 1211 Geneva 20, Switzerland

Information Trends, DSE, Han Bockler Str. 5, 53225 Bonn, Germany

IRED Forum, 3 rue de Varembe, Case 116, 1211 Geneva, Switzerland

Journal of Practice in Development Education, c/o John Turner, University of Manchester, Manchester, M15 4PR, U.K.

LearnTech Forum, EDC, 55 Chapel St., Newton, MA 02160

NCAL Connections, Univ. of Pennsylvania, Philadelphia, PA 19104

NORRAG News, Institut Universitaire d'Etudes du Developpement, Post Box 136, 1211 Geneva, Switzerland

Noticias de la RED, CIDE, Casilla 13608, Santiago 1, Chile

PRODDER, HSRC, P.O. Box 32410, Braamfontein 2107, South Africa

SACHES Newsletter, Dept. of Com. Educ., UWC, Bag X17, Belleville 7535, South Africa

Science Education Newsletter, British Council, Medlock St., Manchester M15 4PR, U.K.

SEAMEO Quarterly, 920 Sukhumvit Rd., Bangkok 10110, Thailand

SEARRAG Bulletin, Unit of Research in Basic Education, Univ. Sains Malaysia, 11800 Penang, Malaysia

Staff Devt. Newsletter, SRIIE, Univ. of Southampton, SO9 5NH, U.K.

UIE Newsletter, Feldbrunnenstr. 58, W-2000 Hamburg 13, Germany

UNESCO Adult Education Information Notes, Basic Educ. Div., UNESCO 7, place de Fontenoy, Paris 75700, France

UNESCO-Africa, Regional Office, 12 Av. Roume, PB 3311, Dakar, Senegal

USCEFA, 1616 North Fort Myer Drive, 11th floor, Arlington, VA 22209

WHE News, HEG, Educ. & Science Div., British Council, Medlock St., Manchester M15 4PR, U.K.

Who's Where in Technology Education, 28 Bruhler Herrenberg, O-5023 Erfurt, Germany

GLOSSARY OF ABBREVIATIONS

AAAS	American Association for the Advancement of Science
ACO	African Curriculum Organization
ACU	Association of Commonwealth Universities
ADEF	Association for the Development of Education and Training in Africa
ADEN	African Development Education Network
AED	Academy for Educational Development
AERN	African Educational Research Network
AFEC	French Comparative Education Society
APEID	Asia and Pacific Programme of Educational Innovation for Development
ASAUK	African Studies Association of the United Kingdom
ASEASUK	Association of Southeast Asian Studies in the United Kingdom
BALID	British Association for Literacy in Development
BATROE	British Association of Teachers and Researchers in Overseas Education
BCIES	British Comparative and International Education Society
BEMAS	British Educational Management and Administration Society
BERA	Botswana Educational Research Association
BERA	British Educational Research Association
BOLESWA	Botswana, Lesotho, and Swaziland Educational Research Association
BRIDGES	Basic Research and Implementation in Developing Education Systems Project
CAERA	Central African Educational Research Association
CAETA	Commonwealth Association for the Education and Training of Adults
CAI	Creative Associates International
CAPA	Commonwealth Association of Polytechnics in Africa
CARNEID	Caribbean Network of Educational Innovation for Development
CASTME	Commonwealth Association of Science, Technology, and Mathematics Educators
CD-ROM	Compact disk, read-only memory

CELADE	Latin American Center for Demographic Studies
CEPAL	Economic Commission for Latin America
CESO	Centre for the Study of Education in Developing Countries
CGECCD	Consultative Group on Early Childhood Care and Development
CIDA	Canadian International Development Agency
CIDE	Center for Educational Research and Development
CIES	Comparative and International Education Society
CINTERFOR-ILO	Regional Office for Latin America of the International Labour Office
CLACSO	Latin American Council for the Study of Social Sciences
CODIESE	Programme of Cooperation in Research and Development for Educational Innovation in South and Southeast Europe
COL	Commonwealth of Learning
ComSec	Commonwealth Secretariat
CREFAL	Latin American Regional Center for Literacy and Adult Education
CRESALC	Center for Trade Union Education, Latin America and Caribbean
DDR	German Democratic Republic
DSA	Developmental Studies Association
DSE	German Foundation for International Development
EAC	East African Community
EARLI	European Network for Research on Learning and Instruction
EC	European Community
EIPDAS	Educational Innovation Programme for Development in the Arab States
ERNESA	Educational Research Network in Eastern and Southern Africa
ERNETA	Educational Research Network of Tanzania
ERNIKE	Educational Research Network in Kenya
ERNWACA	Educational Research Network for Western and Central Africa
FEMNET	African Women Development and Communication Network
FRG	Federal Republic of Germany
HIID	Harvard Institute for International Development
IBE	International Bureau of Education
ICAE	International Council for Adult Education
ICDE	International Council for Distance Education
IDE	InerAmerican Development Bank
IDRC	International Development Research Centre
IEA	International Education Achievement
IERS	International Education Reporting Service
ILDEP	Indonesian Linguistic Development Project
ILO	International Labour Office
INEADE	National Institute for the Development of Education
INED	International Network for Educational Information
ISFRA	Superior Institute for Training and Applied Research
KUTERA	Kenya, Uganda, Tanzania Educational Research Association
LASA	Latin American Studies Association
LDC	later developing country
NCE	National Commission on Education
NCLD	Indonesian National Centre for Linguistic Development
NEIDA	Network of Educational Innovation for Development in Africa
NGO	nongovernmental organization
NIDMAR	Network for Instruments of Development, Maintenance and Repair

NORRAG	Northern Research, Review, and Advisory Group
NUSESA	Network of Users of Scientific Equipment in Southern Africa
OAS	Organization of American States
ODA	Overseas Development Administration
OEI	Iberoamerican Education Organization
OXFAM	Oxford Famine Relief
PICPEMCE	Regional Network for Teacher Training
PTA	Preferential Trade Area
REDALF	Red de Alfabetización (Literacy Network)
REDUC	Red Latinoamericana de Información y Documentación en Educación
REPLAD	Regional Network for Planning and Administration of Literacy Development
RINAF	Regional Information Network for Africa
ROCARE	Réseau Ouest Central Africain de Recherche en Education
RRAG	Research Review and Advisory Group
RTI	Research Triangle Institute
SACHES	Southern African Comparative and History of Education Society
SADC	Southern Africa Development Community
SEABAS	South East Asia Bibliographic and Abstracting Service
SEAD	Scottish Education Action for Development
SEARRAG	South East Asia Research Review and Advisory Group
SERI	Southern Educational Research Initiative
SIDA	Swedish International Development Agency
SIG	Special Interest Group
SIRI	Regional Information System
STME	Science, Technology and Math Education
SVO	Dutch Council for Educational Research
UCET	Universities Council for the Education of Teachers
UDES	university departments of education
UIE	UNESCO Institute for Education
UKFIET	United Kingdom Forum on International Education and Training
UNECIA	Universities of the North of England Consortium for International Activities
UNESCO	United Nations Educational, Scientific and Cultural Organization
UNICEF	United Nations Children's Fund
USAID	United States Agency for International Development
USDESA	University Staff Development in Eastern and Southern Africa
WCCES	World Council of Comparative Education Societies
WCEFA	World Council on Education for All
WORM	write once, read many

REFERENCES

Adler, N. J. 1986. *International Dimensions of Organizational Behavior.* Boston: Kent.

Argyris, C. 1980. *Inner Contradictions of Rigorous Research.* New York: Academic Press.

Avalos, Beatrice, and Wadi Haddad. 1981. *A Review of Teacher Effectiveness Research in Africa, India, Latin America, Middle East, Malaysia, Philippines and Thailand: Synthesis of Results.* Ottawa: International Development Research Centre.

Bakis, H. 1993. *Les Réseaux et Leurs Enjeux Sociaux.* Paris: PUF.

Barnes, J. A. 1969. "Networks and Political Process." In *Social Networks in Urban Situations,* ed. J. C. Mitchell. Manchester: Published for the Institute for Social Research, University of Zambia, by Manchester University Press.

Bayart, J. F. 1989. *L'Etat en Afrique.* Paris: Fayard.

Bellman, B., and A. Tindumbon. 1991. "Global Networks and International Communication: AFRINET." Paper presented at 1991 annual meeting of African Studies Association, St. Louis, MO.

Bond, M. H. 1991. *Beyond the Chinese Face: Insights from Psychology.* Hong Kong: Oxford.

Bott, E. 1971. *Family and Social Networks: Roles, Norms, and External Relationships in Ordinary Urban Families.* London: Tavistock.

Brunner, J. J. 1993. "La Investigacion Educacional Latinoamericana de Cara al Año 2000." Mimeo. Santiago, Chile: Centro de Investigacion y Desarrollo de la Educación (CIDE).

Callons, M. 1989. *La Science et Ses Réseaux.* Paris: La Découverte.

Cariola, P. 1991. *Factores del Desarrollo Institucional de la Investigacion Educacional en America Latina.* Documento de discusion. Santiago: CIDE. Unpublished.

Cariola, P. 1993. *Relaciones de las ONG-Ministerio de Educacion 1990–1993.* Documento de discusion. Santiago: CEPAL. Unpublished.

Cariola, Patricio, et al. 1987. *Linking Research and Decision Making in Education: The REDUC Network in Latin America.* Ottawa: International Development Research Centre.

Castles, S., H. Klug, and P. Richer, eds. 1981. *Education and Culture for Liberation in Southern Africa: Foundation for Education with Production.* Gaborone, Botswana: Gaborone Printing Works.

CEPAL/UNESCO. 1992. *Educacion y Conocimiento: Eje de la Transformacion Productiva con Equidad*. Santiago: CEPAL.

Cheng, K. M. 1991. "Challenging the North-South Paradigm: Educational Research in East Asia." In *Strengthening Educational Research in Developing Countries*, ed. International Institute for Educational Planning, Paris, and Institute of International Education, Stockholm. Paris: UNESCO/IIEP.

Cheng, K. M. 1993. "Cultural Assumptions Embedded in Networking," *NORRAG News*, 13: 13.

Cheng, K. M. 1994. SERI, A Proposal. Unpublished.

CLASCO/REDUC. 1993. *Propuesta Para Una Agenda de la Investigacion Educacional Latinoamericana de Cara al Año 2000*. Resultado del seminario regional La investigacion Latinoamericana de Cara al Año 2000. Forthcoming.

Coombe, T. 1991. *A Consultation on Higher Education in Africa*. New York: The Ford Foundation.

Crouch, L. A. 1993. *Success in Policy Reform Through Policy Dialogue*. Research Triangle Park, NC: Research Triangle Institute, Center for International Development.

Crouch, L. A., E. Vegas, and R. Johnson. 1993. *Policy Dialogue and Reform in the Education Sector: Necessary Steps and Conditions*. Washington, D.C.: Education and Human Resources Technical Services, U.S. Agency for International Development.

Deleuze, G., and F. Guattari. 1976. *Rhizome: Introduction*. Paris: Editions de Minuit.

Derrida, J. 1972. *Marges*. Paris: Editions de Minuit.

Dore, R. 1976. *The Diploma Disease: Education, Qualification and Development*. Berkeley: University of California Press.

Dubbeldam, L.F.B. 1964. "The Devaluation of the Kapauku-Cowrie as a Factor of Social Disintegration." Part 2. *American Anthropologist* 66, no. 4: 293–322.

Dupuy, G. 1985. *Systèmes, Réseaux, et Territoires*. Paris: Presses de l'Ecole Nationale des Ponts et Chaussées.

Durand, J. P. 1992. Paper presented at Colloquium on Sociology of Research, Yverdon, Switzerland, November 1992.

Edwards, E. and M. P. Todaro. 1974. "Education and Employment in Developing Countries." In *Education and Development Reconsidered*, ed. F. C. Ward. New York: Praeger.

Entwistle, N. 1993. "European Association for Research on Learning and Instruction." *NORRAG News*, 13: 24.

ERNESA. 1990. "The Legal Status of ERNESA." Harare Workshop.

Eshiwani, G. 1991. "Networking in Education." Paper presented at Swaziland Research Association Conference, Manzini, July 29.

Fei, Hsiao-tung. 1981. *Toward a People's Anthropology*. Beijing: New World Press.

Ferrand, A. 1987. *Un Niveau Intermédiaire, les Réseaux Sociaux*. Actes du Séminaire. Paris: CESOL/IRESCO.

Forrester, J. 1988. *Planning in the Face of Power*. Berkeley: University of California Press.

Gallart, M. A. 1993. "Latin American Education and Work Network." *NORRAG News*, 13: 16.

Gmelin, W. 1993. "Networks, Self-Interest & Sustainability." *NORRAG News*, 13: 12.

González Cornejo, Jose. 1992. *Hipertext: Utilizacion en el Tratamiento Documental de Dato: Del M/ISIS al IZE*. 2nd edition. Santiago: Centro de Investigacion y Desarrollo Educativo.

Guralnik, David B. 1976. *Webster's New World Dictionary of the American Language*. New York: Popular Library.

Hallak, J., and A. Tobelem. 1993. *IIEP Newsletter*, 11, no. 1. Paris.

Hanks, P., ed. 1979. *Collins Dictionary of the English Language*. London: Collins.

Hoare, Q., and G. N. Smith, eds. 1971. *Selections from the Prison Notebooks of Antonio Gramsci.* New York: International Publishers.

Hochleitner Diez, R. 1978. *The Spanish Educational Reform and Lifelong Education.* Study prepared for the UNESCO Institute of Education in collaboration with the International Education Reporting Service. Paris: UNESCO.

Hofstede, G. 1984. *Culture's Consequences: International Differences in Work-Related Values.* Abridged edition. Beverly Hills, CA: Sage.

Husén, T., L. Saha, and R. Noonan. 1978. *Teacher Training and Student Achievement in Less Developed Countries.* Staff working paper no. 310. Washington, D.C.: World Bank.

International Development Research Centre. 1976. *Education Research Priorities: A Collective View.* Ottawa: International Development Research Centre.

International Development Research Centre. 1987. *Educational Research Review and Advisory Group: A Description.* Ottawa: International Development Research Centre.

King, Kenneth. 1987. "Donor-Aided Research and Evaluation: The Education Research Program of IDRC." Mimeo. Edinburgh: Edinburgh University Education Department.

King, Kenneth. 1991a. "NORRAG: A Review of the First Four Years, 1986–1990." Mimeo. Edinburgh: Edinburgh University, Education Department.

King, Kenneth. 1991b. *Aid and Education in the Developing World.* London: Longman, Harlow.

Kinyanjui, K. 1990. "The Crisis in Educational Research Capacity in African Universities." Paper presented to Meeting of Donors to African Education, Accra.

Komba, D. 1990. "Educational Research Networking in Eastern and Southern Africa: Opportunities, Challenges and Prospects." In *Educational Research in the SADCC Region: Present and Future.* ed. Gaontatlhe Mautle and Frank Youngman. Gaborone, Botswana: Botswana Educational Research Association.

Komba, D. 1992. "The Concept and Problems of Networking in Educational Research: The Experience of ERNESA." In *Networking in Educational Research,* ed. Barnabas M. Dlamini, Malangeni J. Simelane, and Sihle Zwane. Kwaluseni, Tanzania: SERA.

Landier, H. 1991. *Vers l'entreprise intelligente.* Paris: Calmann-Levy.

Levey, L. 1993. Report to donors to African Education Working Group on Higher Education, Dar es Salaam, September 21–22.

Malinowski, B. 1950. *Argonauts of the Western Pacific.* New York: E. P. Dutton.

May, N. 1992. "Organisation Productive et Réseaux." Paper presented at Colloquium on Sociology of Research, Yverdon, Switzerland, November 1992.

Meister, A. 1978. *La Participation pour le Développement.* Paris: Anthropos.

Miller, E. 1983. "Research Environment in the English-Speaking Caribbean." In *Educational Research Environments in the Developing World.* ed. S. Shaeffer and J. A. Nkinyangi. Ottawa: International Development Research Centre.

Ministry of Education and Culture, Republic of Malawi. 1985. *Education Development Plan 1985–1995: A Summary.* Zomba: Malawi Institute of Education.

Mitchell, J. Clyde. 1969. *Social Networks in Urban Situations: Analyses of Personal Relationships in Central African Towns.* Manchester, UK: University of Manchester Press, published for the University of Zambia.

Moreno, J. L. 1934. *Who Shall Survive? A New Approach to the Problem of Human Interrelations.* Washington, D.C.: Nervous and Mental Disease Publishing.

Mulgan, G. J. 1991. *Communication and Control: Networks and the New Economics of Communication.* Cambridge, UK: Polity Press.

Myers, R. G. 1981. *Connecting Worlds: A Summary of Developments in Educational Research in Latin America.* Ottawa: International Development Research Centre.

Namuddu, Katherine, and S. Tapsoba. 1993. *The Status of Educational Research and Policy Analysis in Sub-Saharan Africa: A Report of the DAE Working Group on Capacity Building in Educational Research and Policy Analysis.* Dakar, Senegal: IERC, Nanobi.

NORRAG News. 1986. No. 1. Stockholm: University of Stockholm.

NORRAG News. 1992. No. 13, *Special Issue: Networking in Education and Training.* Edinburgh: Edinburgh University Centre for African Studies.

NORRAG. 1992. *Statutes.* Geneva: Institut Universitaire d'Etudes du Développement.

Nyati-Ramahobo, Lydia, and B. Prophet. n.d. "The Application of Educational Research to Policy Making: Problems and Possibilities." *Modenodi* 1, no. 1: 39.

Odedra-Straub, M. 1992. *Much More Than Human Resource Development for Africa: Key Issues for Developing Countries.* London: Tata McGraw-Hill.

Parsons, Q. N. 1983. "Education and Development in Pre-Colonial and Colonial Botswana to 1965." In *Education for Development: Proceedings of a Symposium Held by the Botswana Society at the National Museum and Art Gallery.* ed. Michael Crowder. Gaborone, Botswana: Macmillan.

Peresuh, M. 1993. "Educational Research Priorities in the SADC Region." Keynote address to the BERA National Seminar on Determining Educational Research Priorities for National Development Plan 7. June 7–8, 1993, Gaborone, Botswana.

Piddington, R. 1950. *An Introduction to Social Anthropology.* New York: Praeger.

Poposil, Leopold. 1954. "Kapauku Papuans and their Law." *Yale University Publications in Anthropology,* no. 44, New Haven.

Pritchard, C. 1978. "Informal Networks and their Properties: A State-of-the-Art Review for RRAG." Mimeo. Ottawa: International Development Research Centre.

Psacharopoulos, G. 1990. "Comparative Education: From Theory to Practice, or Are You a:\neo.* or b:*.ist?" *Comparative Education Review* 34, no. 3: 369–390.

Pye, L. W. 1985. *Asian Power and Politics: The Cultural Dimensions of Authority.* Cambridge, MA: Harvard University Press.

Redding, S. G. 1990. *The Spirit of Chinese Capitalism.* Berlin: W. de Gruyter.

Reich, Robert. 1991. *The Work of Nations.* New York: Vintage.

Republic of Botswana. 1977. *National Policy on Education: Government Paper no. 1 of 1977.* Approved by the National Assembly, August, Gaborone, Botswana.

Rojas, A. 1992. *Informacion y Toma de Decisiones en Educacion. Un Estudio de Casos.* Santiago: UNESCO/REDUC.

Ronen, S. 1986. *Comparative and Multi-National Management.* New York: John Wiley & Sons.

Serres, M. 1968. *La Communication.* Paris: Ediciones de Minuit.

Shaeffer, S., and J. A. Nkinyangi, eds. 1983. *Educational Research Environments in the Developing World.* Ottawa: International Development Research Centre.

Shaw, S. A. F. 1989. "The Historical Development of Primary Education in Botswana as a Two-Tier System." Paper presented at the BOLESWA Education Research Symposium in the SADC Region, held at the University of Botswana, Gaborone.

Von Laue, T. H. 1987. *The World Revolution of Westernization: The Twentieth Century in Global Perspective.* New York: Oxford University Press.

Ward, F. C., ed. 1974. *Education and Development Reconsidered: The Bellagio Conference Papers.* New York: Praeger.

Watson, K. 1993. "Professional Associations and Academic Networks: The UK." *NORRAG News,* 13: 38–42.

World Bank. 1974. *Education: Sector Working Paper.* Washington, D.C.: World Bank.

World Bank. 1988. *Education in Sub-Saharan Africa: Policies for Adjustment, Revitalization and Expansion.* Washington, D.C.: World Bank.

INDEX OF PERSONS

INDEX OF TOPICS

ABOUT THE EDITOR
AND CONTRIBUTORS

EDITOR

NOEL F. McGINN is Professor of Education, Harvard University Graduate School of Education, and Fellow, Harvard Institute for International Development. He is the current President of the Northern Policy, Review, Research, and Advisory Group (NORRAG). Most of his professional work has been on how to assist education leaders to make decisions informed by research. With Allison Borden he recently published *Framing Questions, Constructing Answers: Linking Research with Education Policy for Developing Countries.*

CONTRIBUTORS

PETER BADCOCK-WALTERS is Executive Director of the Education Foundation, a leading nongovernment policy and information systems support institute in South Africa. He is currently involved in the establishment of provincial EMIS units and in South Africa's first school location database, including a detailed school register of needs. Badcock-Walters has written extensively on research and policy issues.

PATRICIO CARIOLA, S.J., is Director of the Center for Educational Research and Development (CIDE) in Santiago, Chile, and President of REDUC, the Latin American Network for Education Research. He recently published a chapter in Alvarez and Gomez, *Laying the Foundations: Institutions of Knowledge in Developing Countries.*

MICHEL CARTON has been coordinator of the Northern Policy, Review, Research, and Advisory Group (NORRAG) since 1992 and is currently Deputy Director of the Graduate Institute of Development Studies at Geneva University. His current fields of training and research include training policies in French-speaking Africa, Indonesia, and Vietnam. He was a contributor to the 1994 volume, edited by Joel Samoff, *Coping with Crisis: Austerity, Adjustment and Human Resources.*

CHENG KAI-MING is Dean of Education at the University of Hong Kong. He works in the areas of educational administration, planning, and policy analysis with a research interest focused primarily on the Chinese mainland and other Chinese communities in East Asia. He is currently chair of the Southern Education Research Initiative (SERI), which has liaisons with six regional networks over Africa, Asia, Latin America, and the Caribbean.

LEO F. DUBBELDAM is Director of the Centre for the Study of Education in Developing Countries (CESO) and Professor of Education in Developing Countries at Utrecht University. His current research programs include a literacy project in Ghana, basic and vocational education in South Africa, evaluation of international education programs in Africa and South East Asia, and studies on the relation between education and culture. He is the editor and author of two chapters in the International Yearbook of Education, vol. 44 (1994).

EDUCATION TEAM AT THE COMMONWEALTH SECRETARIAT plays a coordinating role with respect to issues raised at Commonwealth Ministers of Education Conferences, and contributes to programs of professional development in education. Their expertise includes head teacher management, distance education, science education, teacher preparation, and nonformal education.

NOEL ENTWISTLE is Bell Professor of Education and Director of the Centre for Research on Learning and Instruction at the University of Edinburgh. His current research involves the nature of academic understanding and the development of hypertext-based advice on study skills. He edits the journal *Higher Education.*

ZAINAL GHANI is Coordinator for the Unit for Research on Basic Education at University Science Malaysia which develops teaching approaches and materials for rural primary schools in East Malaysia. Among his recent publications is "Student Teachers' Personal Perception of Teaching" with A. Lourdesamy in Ho Wah Kam and Ruth Y. L. Wong, *Improving the Quality of the Teaching Profession: An International Perspective* (1991).

RICHARD GILBERT is a doctoral candidate in International/Intercultural Education at the University of Southern California School of Education. His areas of interest are biotechnology, educational technology, research and evaluation methods, and development education in southern Africa. His work experience has included teaching, research, and consulting for USAID, the National Science Foundation, and other organizations.

DAVID GILMOUR is a Senior Lecturer in the School of Education, University of Cape Town. His recent research projects include evaluations of compensatory education programs in the Western Cape, South Africa. He has published with C. A. Soudien, "Disadvantage in South African Education: The Issue of Transformative Policy and Research" in Donald and Dawes, *Childhood and Adversity in South Africa* (1994).

WOLFGANG GMELIN is affiliated with the German Foundation for International Development (DSE), an institution involved in the further training of specialists and executive personnel from developing countries. His research has focused on cooperation issues in the fields of science and technology, higher education development, and more recently with aspects of capacity building in educational research.

JOSÉ GONZÁLEZ CORNEJO is Associate Professor of Mathematical Models in the Master of Regional Economics at the University Austral of Valdivia, Chile. He is an author, manager, and instructor of personnel involved in a range of computer systems in Europe and Latin America. His research interests focus on the field of hypertext and information management systems.

LINDA GRAY is Director of Scottish Education and Action for Development (SEAD), a membership organization with a focus on the common experiences of development issues in Scotland.

WIM HOPPERS is a former senior researcher and consultant at the Centre for the Study of Education in Developing Countries (CESO). He has worked in teacher education and nonformal vocational training in Africa and has written widely on these subjects, including *Beyond Jomtien: Implementing Primary Education for All* (1994) with Angela Little and Roy Gardner. He is currently stationed in Harare, Zimbabwe as a regional education adviser for the Netherlands government and is directly involved in new initiatives in basic education development.

WOLFGANG KARCHER is a Professor of Education at the Technical University of Berlin. His research and writing are focused in the areas of education and society in Indonesia and out-of-school education and work in the informal sector in less industrialized countries.

KENNETH KING is the Director of the Centre of African Studies, Professor of International and Comparative Education at the University of Edinburgh, and editor of *NORRAG News*. He has researched and published widely in the areas of aid policy toward subsectors of education, technical and vocational education and training, science and technology education, and education and training in microenterprises and the informal sector.

DONATUS KOMBA is Senior Lecturer in the Philosophy of Education and Teacher Education, University of Dar Es Salaam. He was the second coordinator of ERNESA, the Education Research Network for Eastern and Southern Africa, and coordinator of a network on Education with Production in Theory and Action. With Wim Biervliet he edited CESO Paperback No. 21, *Productive Work in Education and Training, a State-of-the-Art in Eastern Africa.*

JON LAUGLO is Professor of Sociology at the University of Trondheim, Norway. His current research on education relates to decentralization policies, vocational training, uses of research in policy making, and the school experience of immigrant children. He is the author of several books on education and has published articles in *Comparative Education Review* and *Comparative Education.*

CHANGU MANNATHOKO is a lecturer in the Department of Educational Foundations at the University of Botswana. Among her recent publications are an article in the *British Journal of Sociology of Education* and *Visions of Teacher Education in Southern Africa: The Botswana Experience* (1995) with C. Yandila.

ROBERT MYERS is coordinator of the Consultative Group on Early Childhood Care and Development, a mechanism for gathering, synthesizing, and disseminating information about child care and development programs in the Third World. In addition to numerous articles, papers, and reviews, his writings include *The Twelve Who Survive* (1992) and *A Fair Start for Children* (1990).

KATHERINE NAMUDDU is currently a Senior Scientist at the Rockefeller Foundation, working on issues of female participation in education. She has taught at Makerere University, Uganda, and the University of Nairobi and Kenyatta University, Kenya.

LYDIA NYATI-RAMAHOBO is head of the Department of Primary Education at the University of Botswana. She has carried out three major studies on gender in education, resulting in a publication by UNICEF titled *The Girl-Child in Botswana: Educational Prospects and Constraints.*

MILTON E. PLOGHOFT is Professor of Education at Ohio University in Athens, Ohio, and serves as Research Fellow and Northern Coordinator of the African Educational Research Network (AERN). He has published articles dealing with electronic information exchange and African university development in the *FID News Bulletin* (1994) and the *Journal of Practice in Development Education* (1995).

MARK RICHMOND has worked for UNESCO's Programme for Education for Emergencies and Reconstruction (PEER) since 1994 and is currently the acting head of UNESCO-PEER in Nairobi, Kenya. He has written extensively on Latin American education with a particular focus on Chile and Cuba and in 1994 coedited the volume *Politics and the Curriculum.*

WILLIAM RIDEOUT, JR., is a Professor and Program Leader of International and Intercultural Education at the University of Southern California and serves as a consultant to the Educational Research Network for Western and Central Africa (ERNWACA). Most recently he coauthored, with Ipek Ural, a study on "Centralization and Decentralization Models of Education: Comparative Studies," published by the Development Bank of South Africa.

ERNESTO SCHIEFELBEIN is the Director of the UNESCO Regional Office of Education for Latin America and the Caribbean. Since 1992 he has been successfully experimenting with personalized and cooperative self-learning approaches in five Latin American countries. He has published two books on this topic, *The State of Education in LAC, 1980–1989* (1992) and *Redefining Basic Education for Latin America* (1992).

DANIEL N. SIFUNA is a Professor in the Department of Educational Foundations, Kenyatta University, Nairobi, Kenya. His current research focuses on the issues of access and equity in Kenya's Public University. He has coauthored an article in the *Journal of Third World Studies* and was a contributor in Mwiria and Wamahiu, *Issues in Educational Research in Africa* (1995).

JUAN CARLOS TEDESCO is the Director of the International Bureau of Education (IBE), Geneva. His research projects in the field of comparative education include teachers and multicultural education, educational research and decision making, and education for citizenship. His most recent publication, coauthored with Ernesto Schiefelbein, is *A New Opportunity* (1995).

KEITH WATSON is Professor of Comparative and International Education at the University of Reading in the United Kingdom and Director of the Centre for International Studies in Education Management and Training. His current research focuses on private faith-based schooling and parental choice. He is the author of several books on educational development.

ISBN 0-275-95511-7

90000>

9 780275 955113

HARDCOVER BAR CODE